the Lady ParaNorma

Written and illustrated by Vincent Marcone

CHIZINE PUBLICATIONS

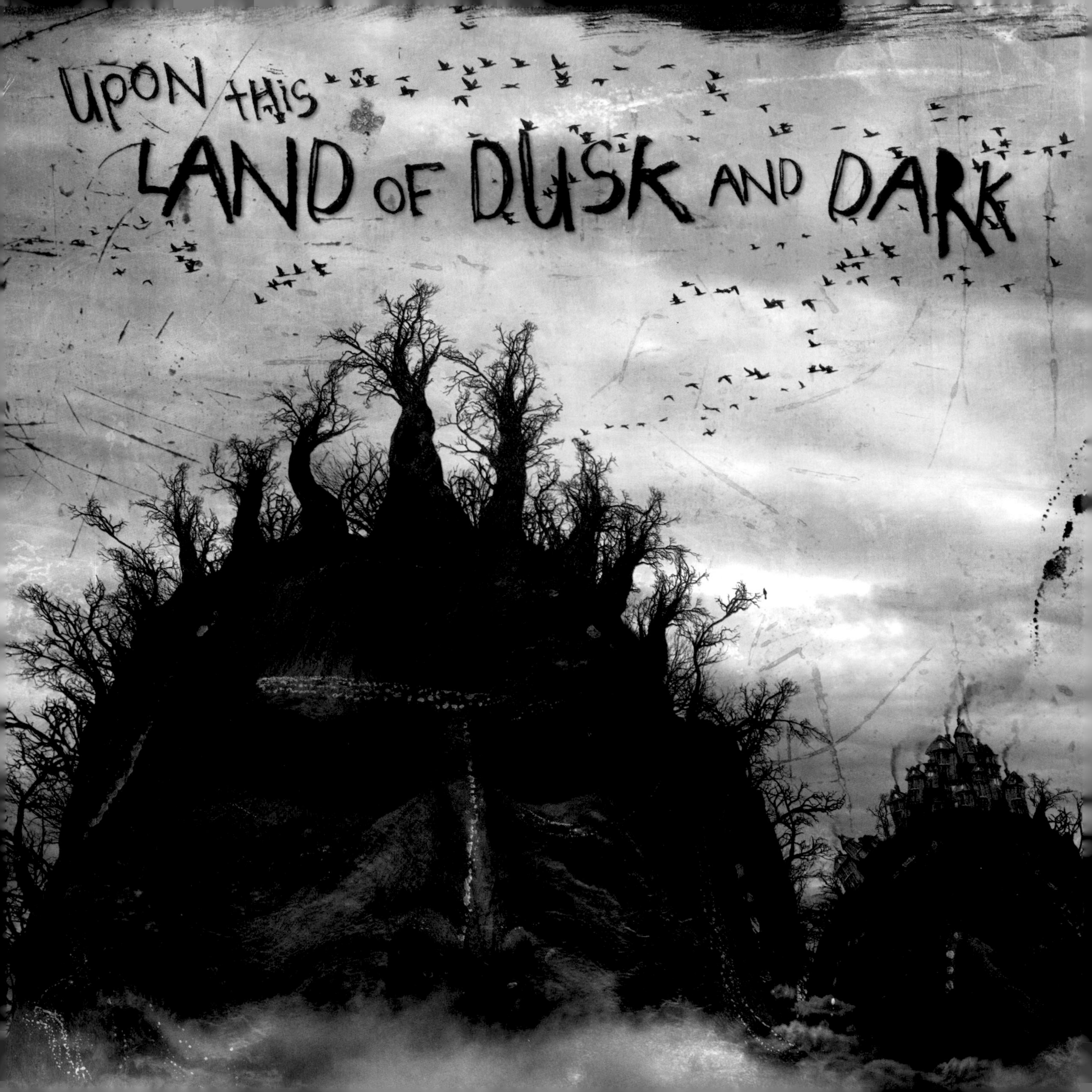
UPON THIS
LAND OF DUSK AND DARK

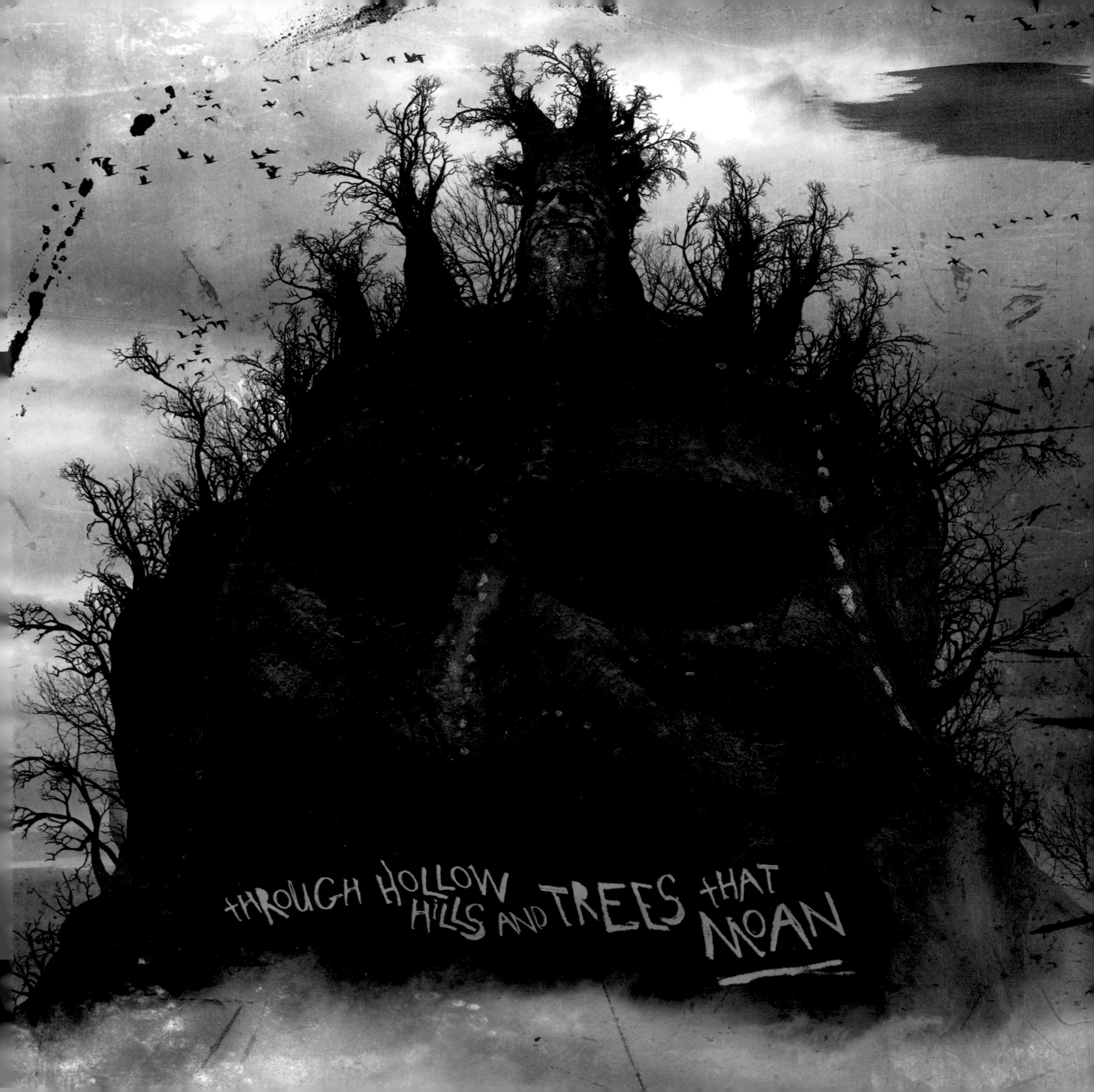
THROUGH HOLLOW HILLS AND TREES THAT MOAN

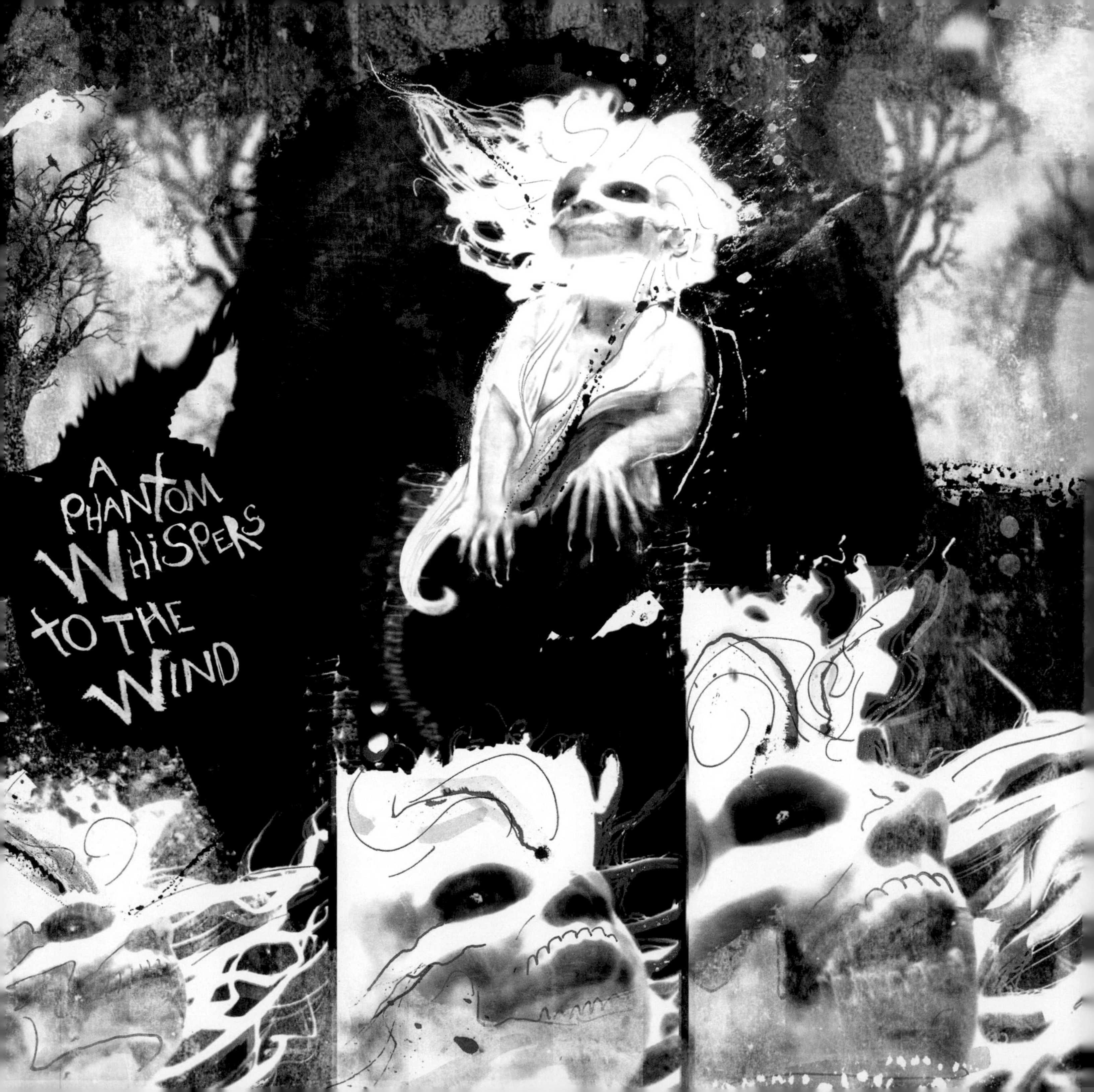
A PHANTOM WHISPERS TO THE WIND

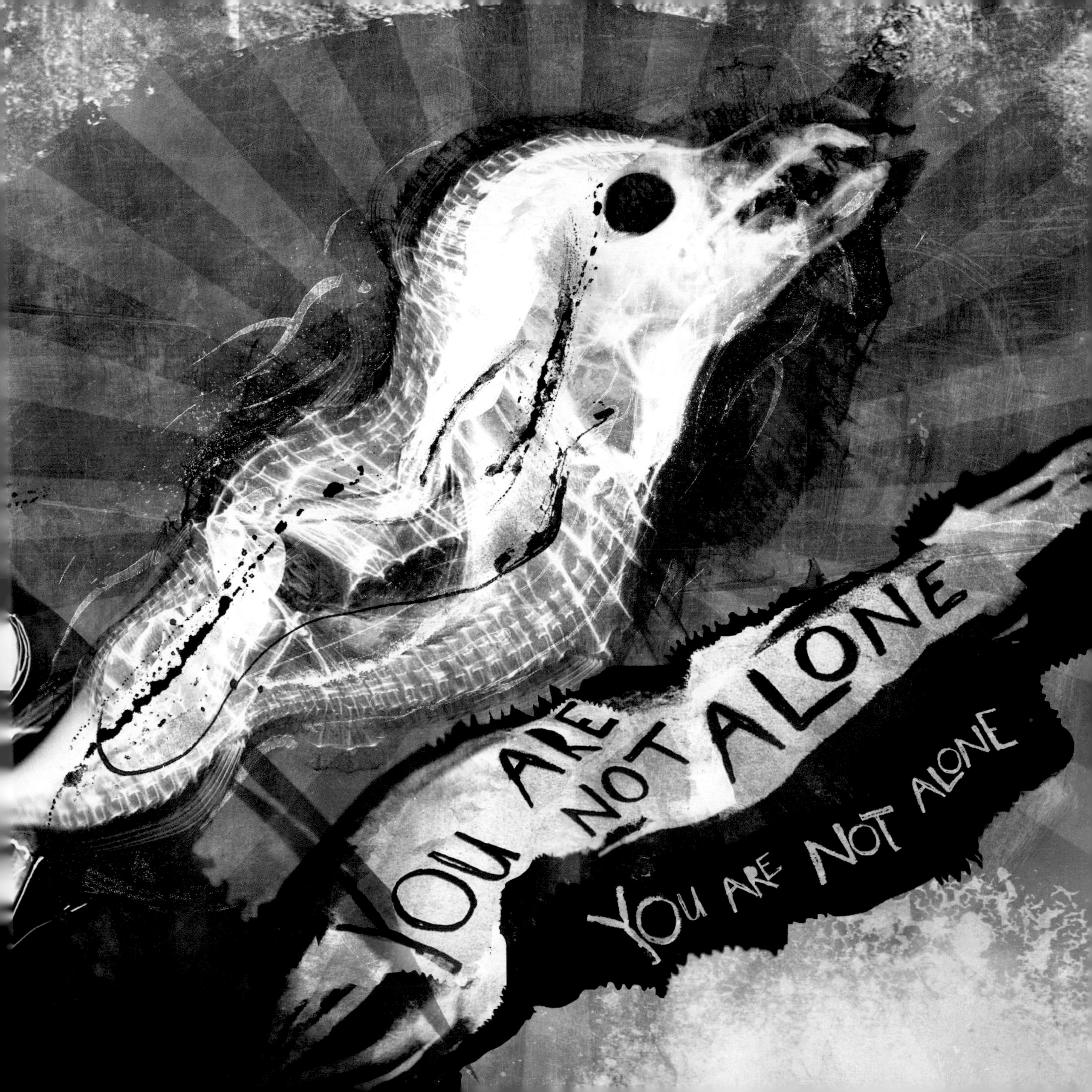
YOU ARE NOT ALONE
YOU ARE NOT ALONE

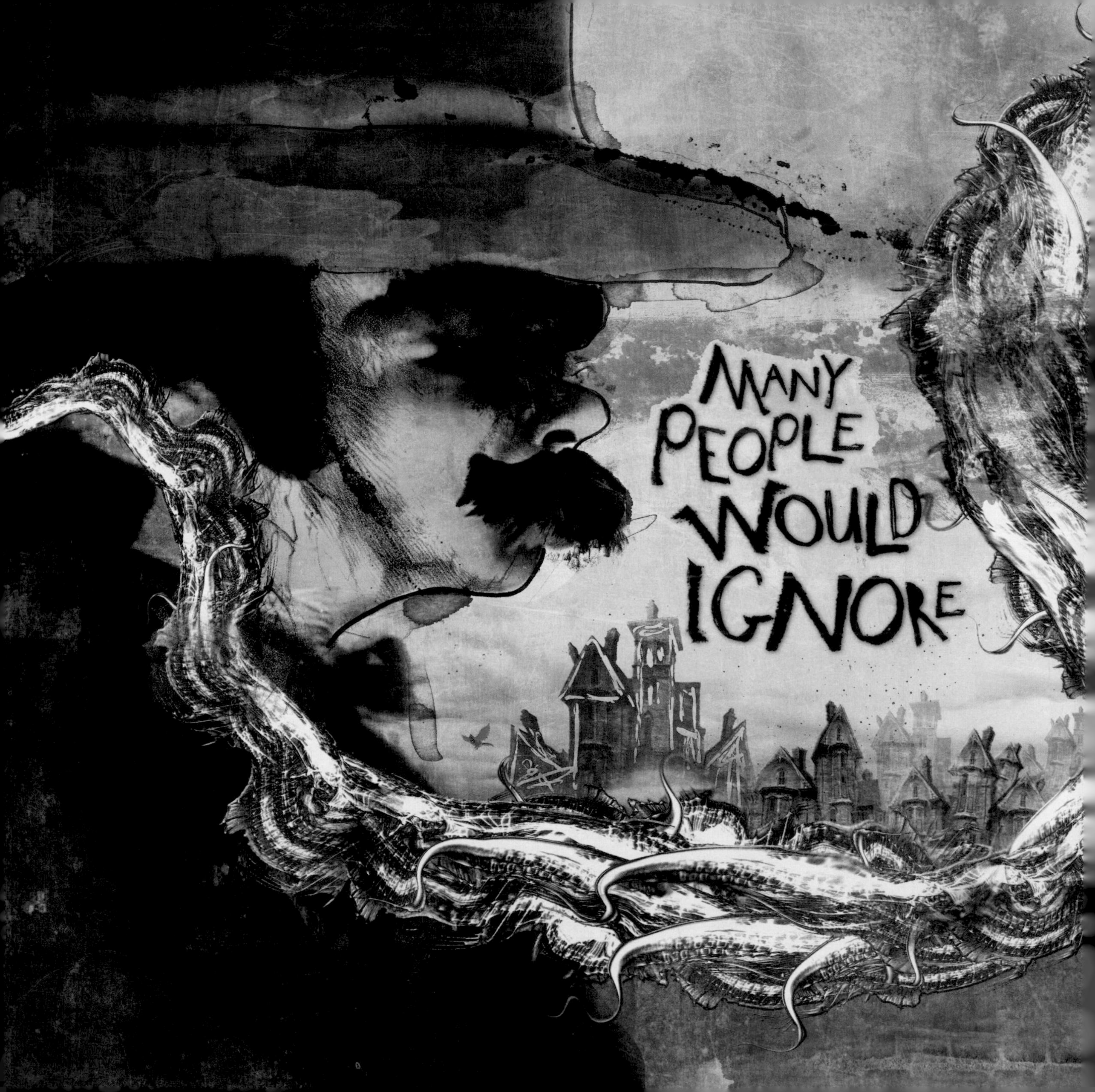
MANY
PEOPLE
WOULD
IGNORE

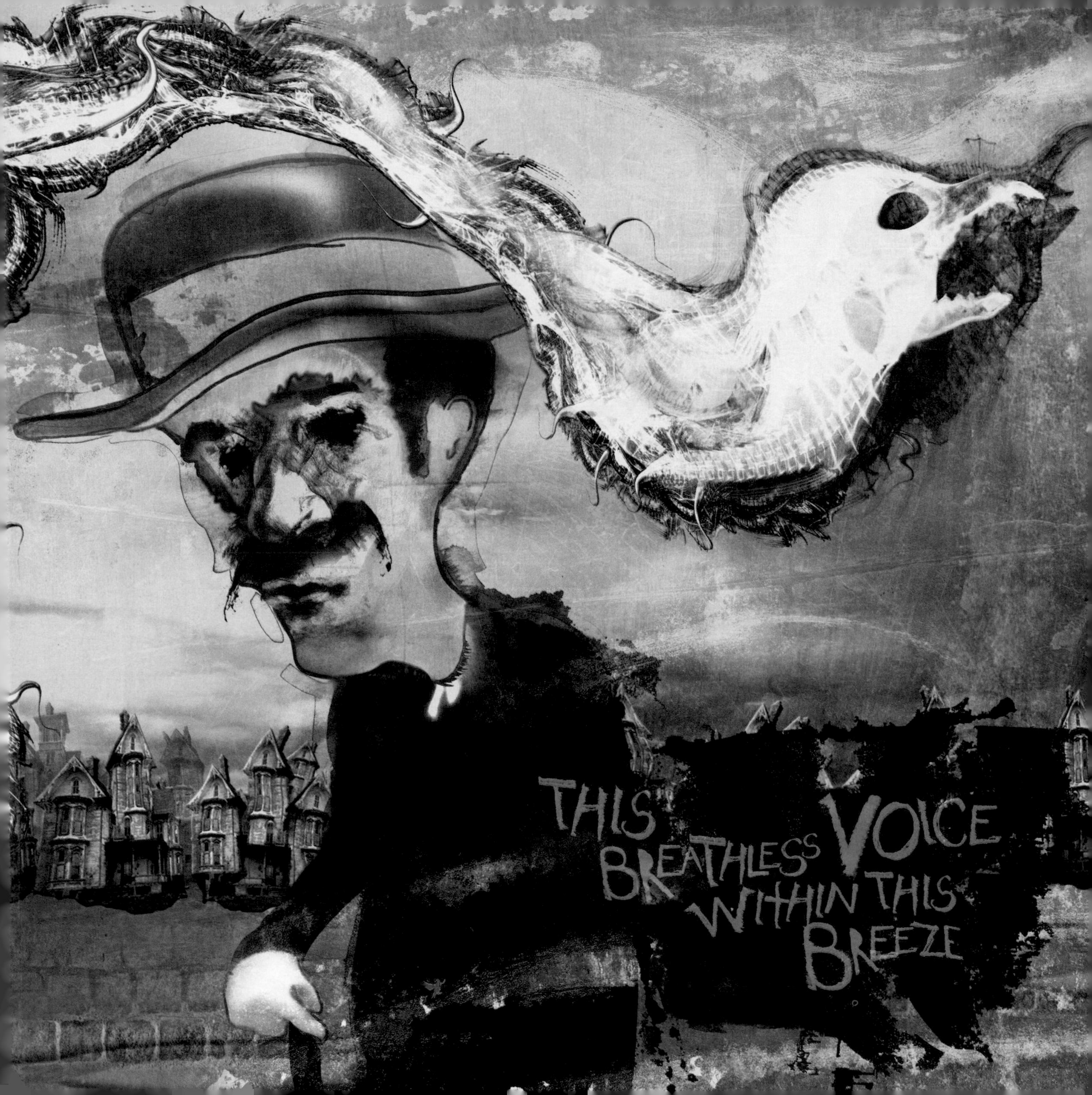
THIS BREATHLESS VOICE
WITHIN THIS
BREEZE

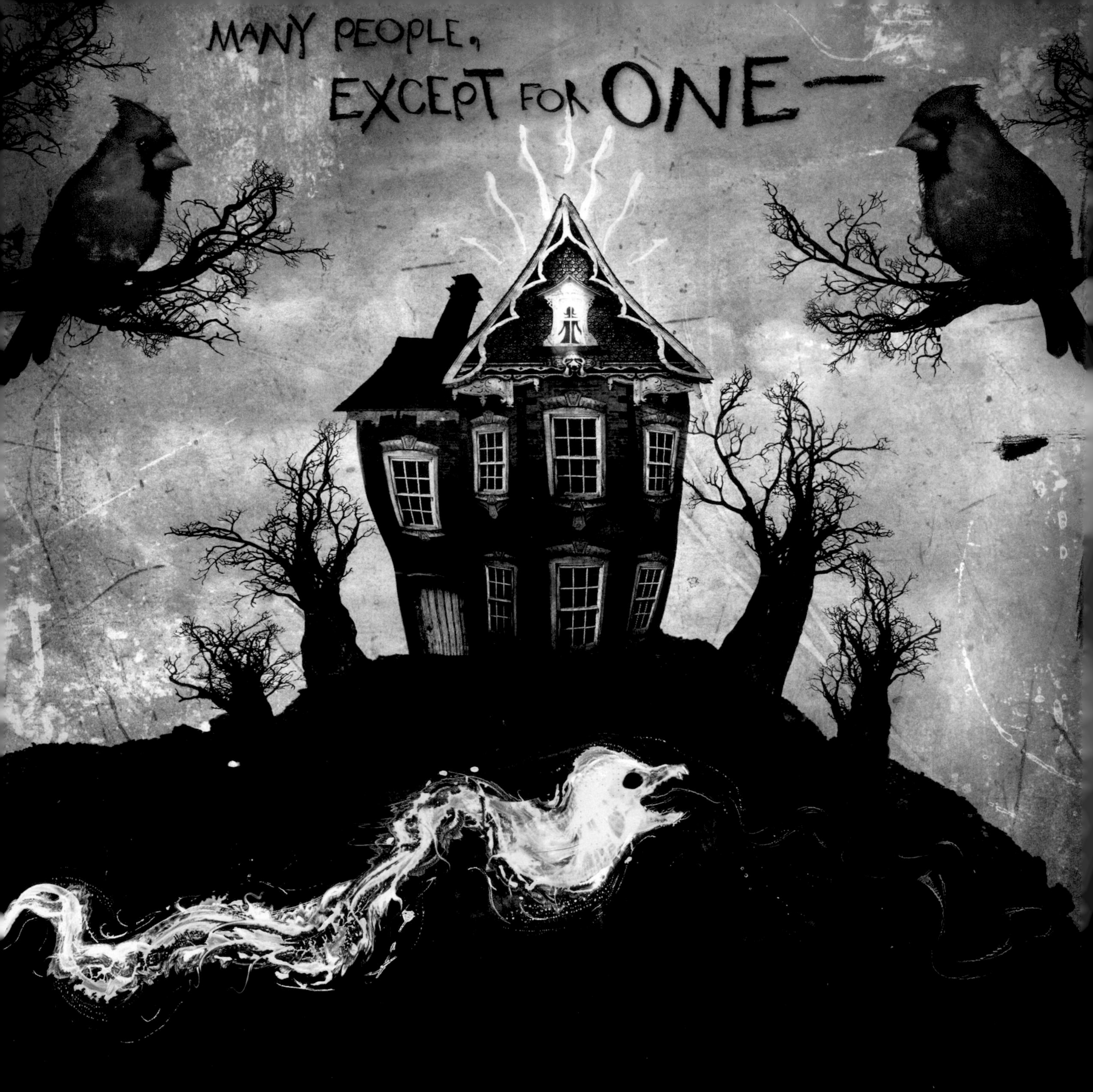
MANY PEOPLE,
EXCEPT FOR ONE—

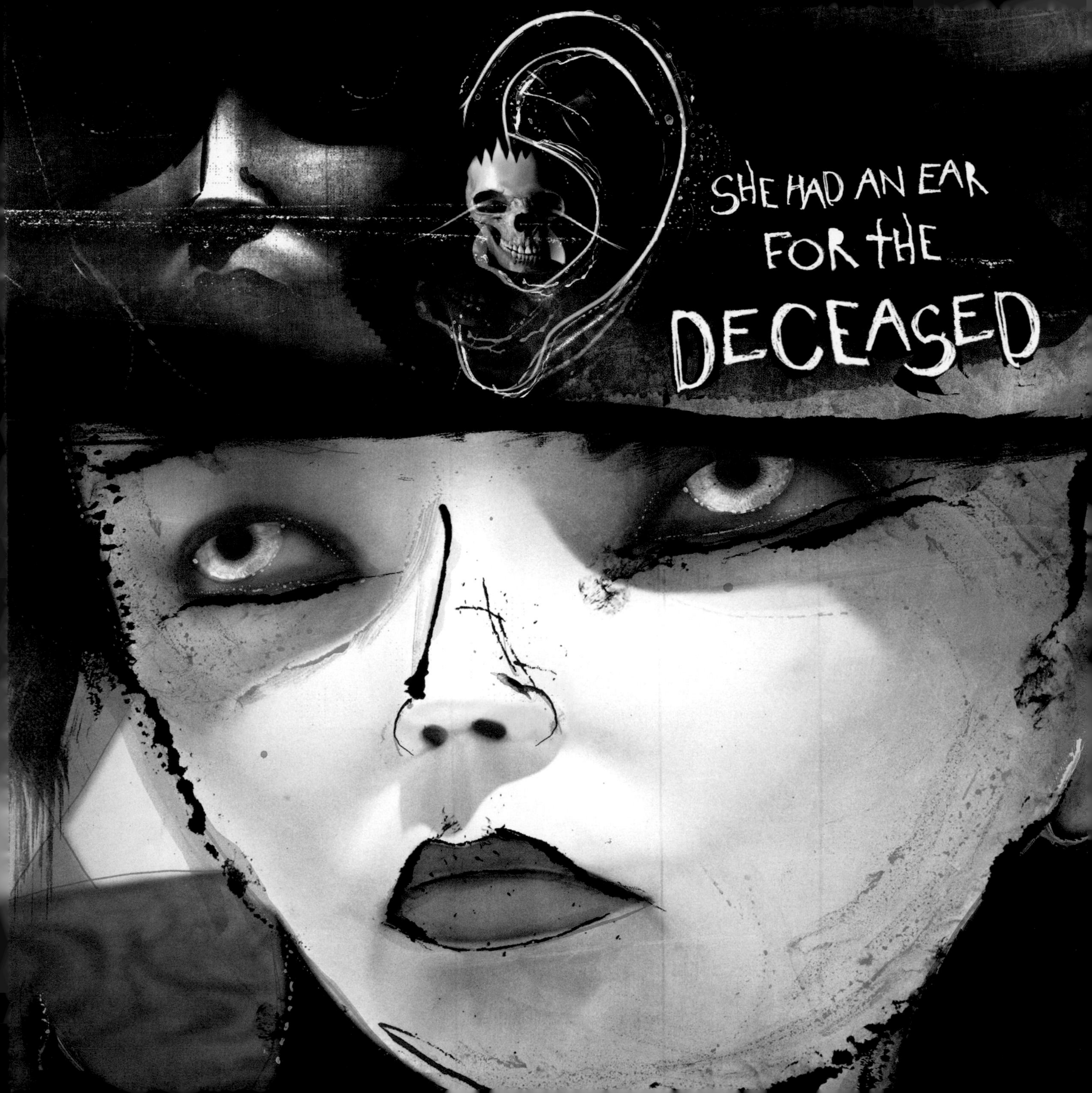
SHE HAD AN EAR FOR THE DECEASED

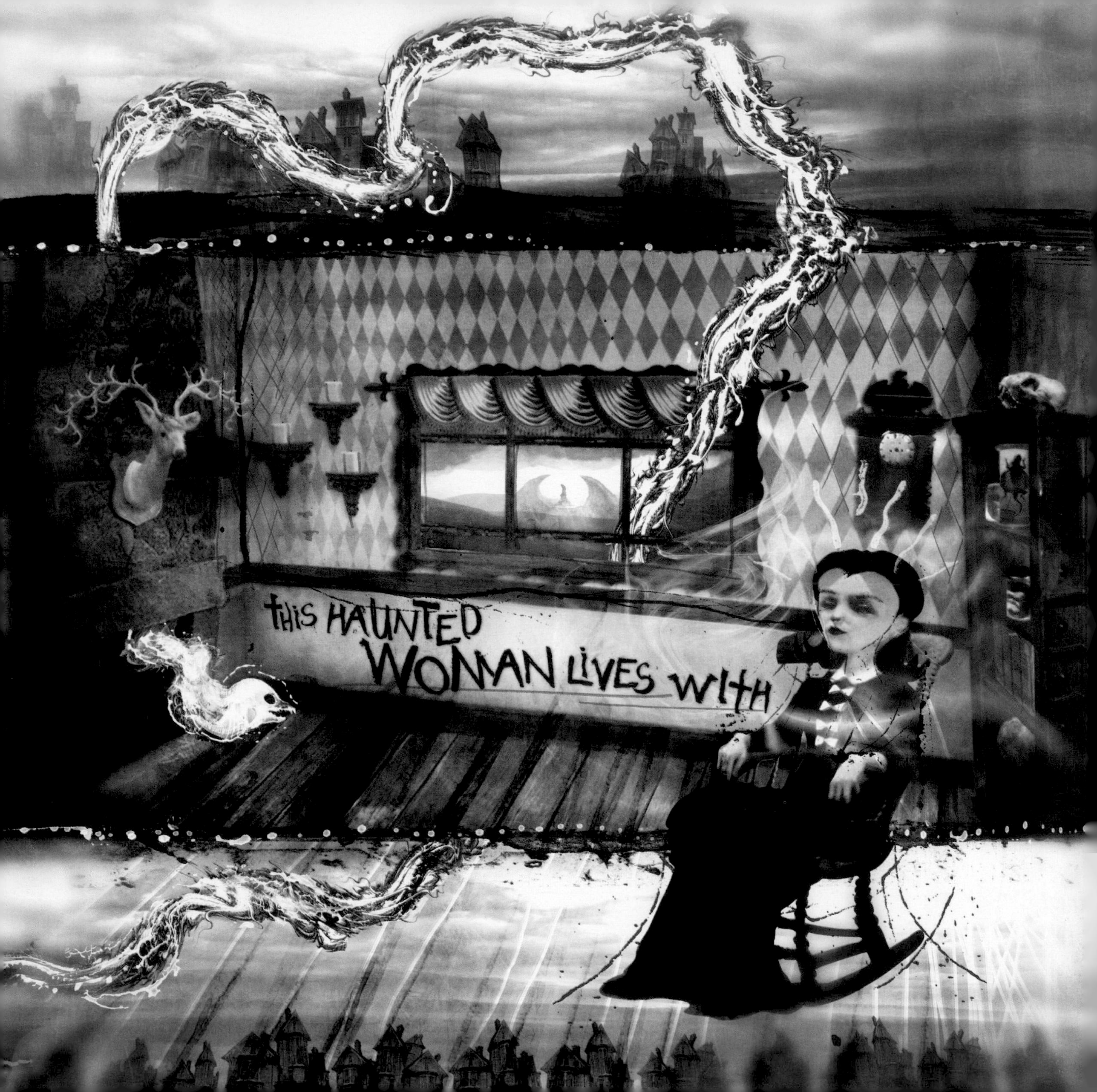
THIS HAUNTED WOMAN LIVES WITH

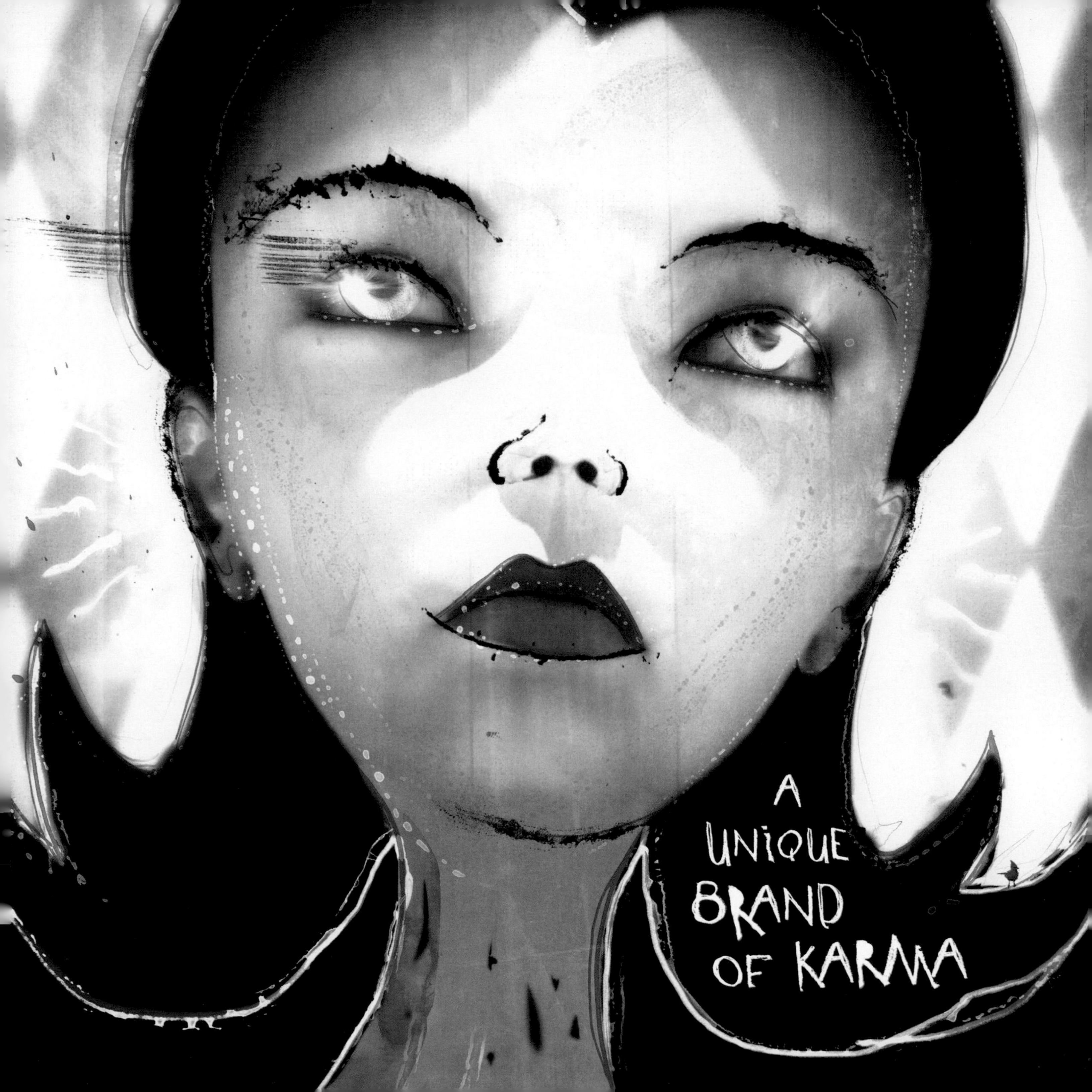
A
UNIQUE
BRAND
OF KARMA

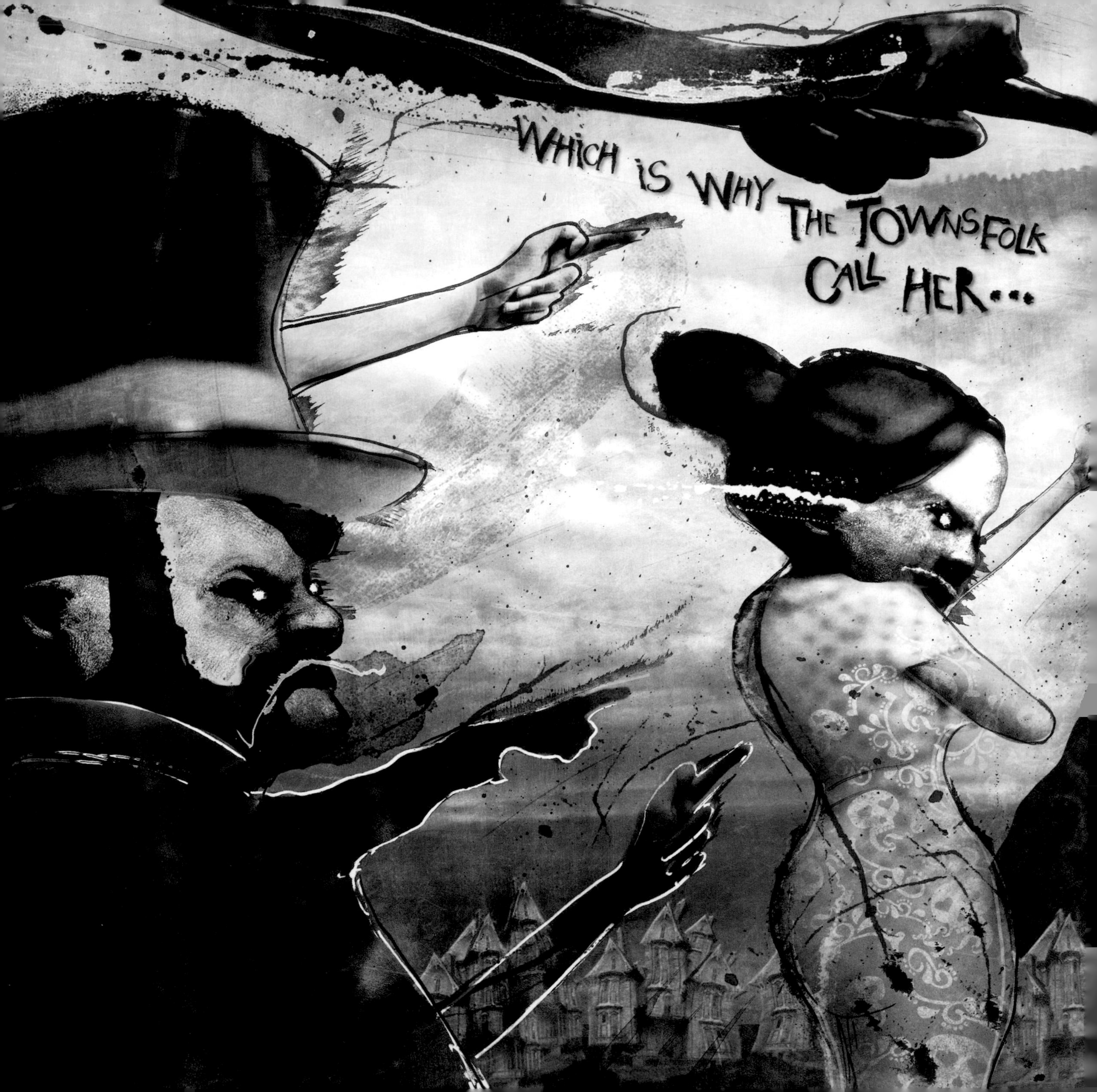
WHICH IS WHY THE TOWNSFOLK CALL HER...

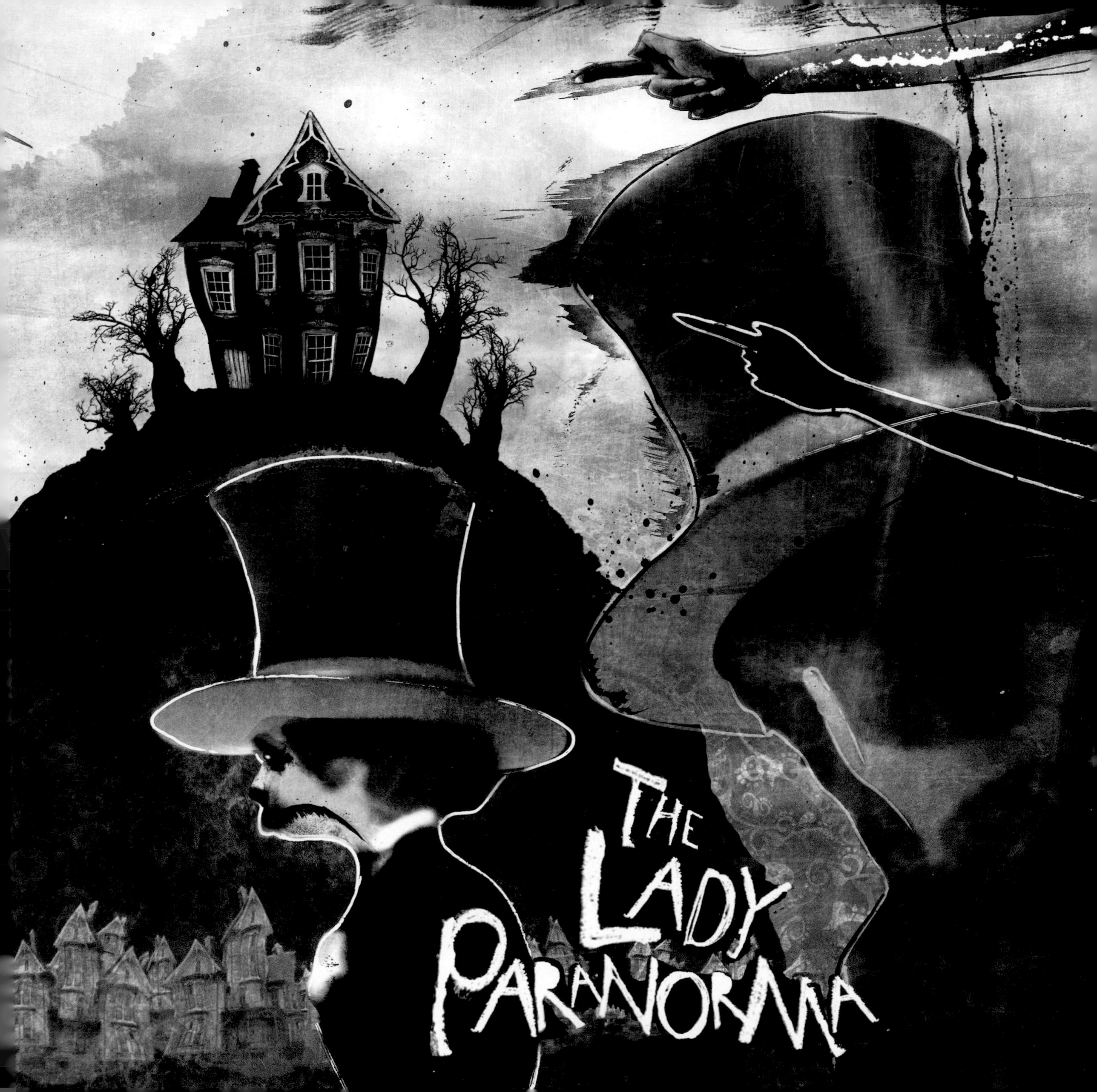
THE
LADY
PARANORMA

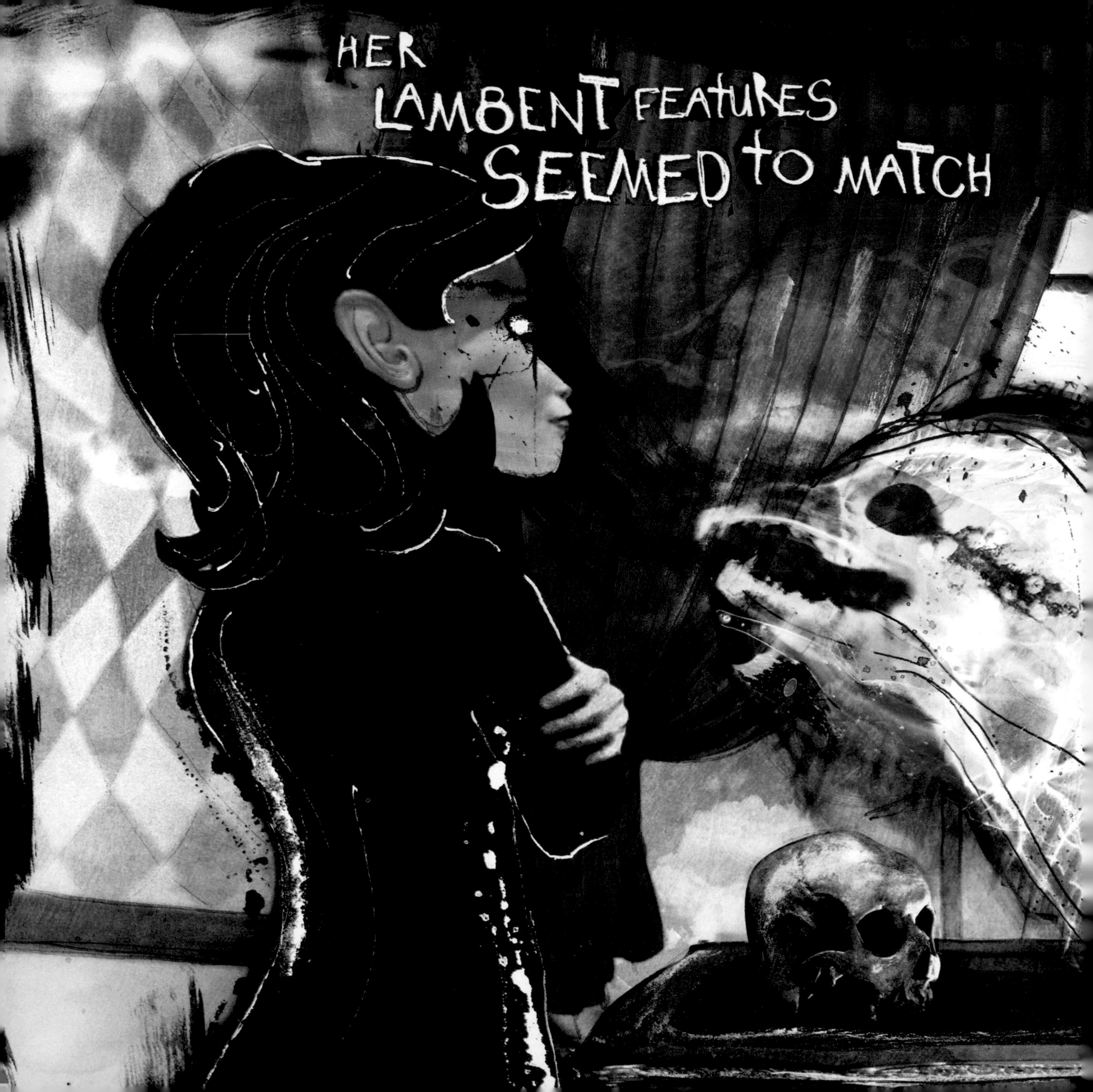
HER
LAMBENT FEATURES
SEEMED TO MATCH

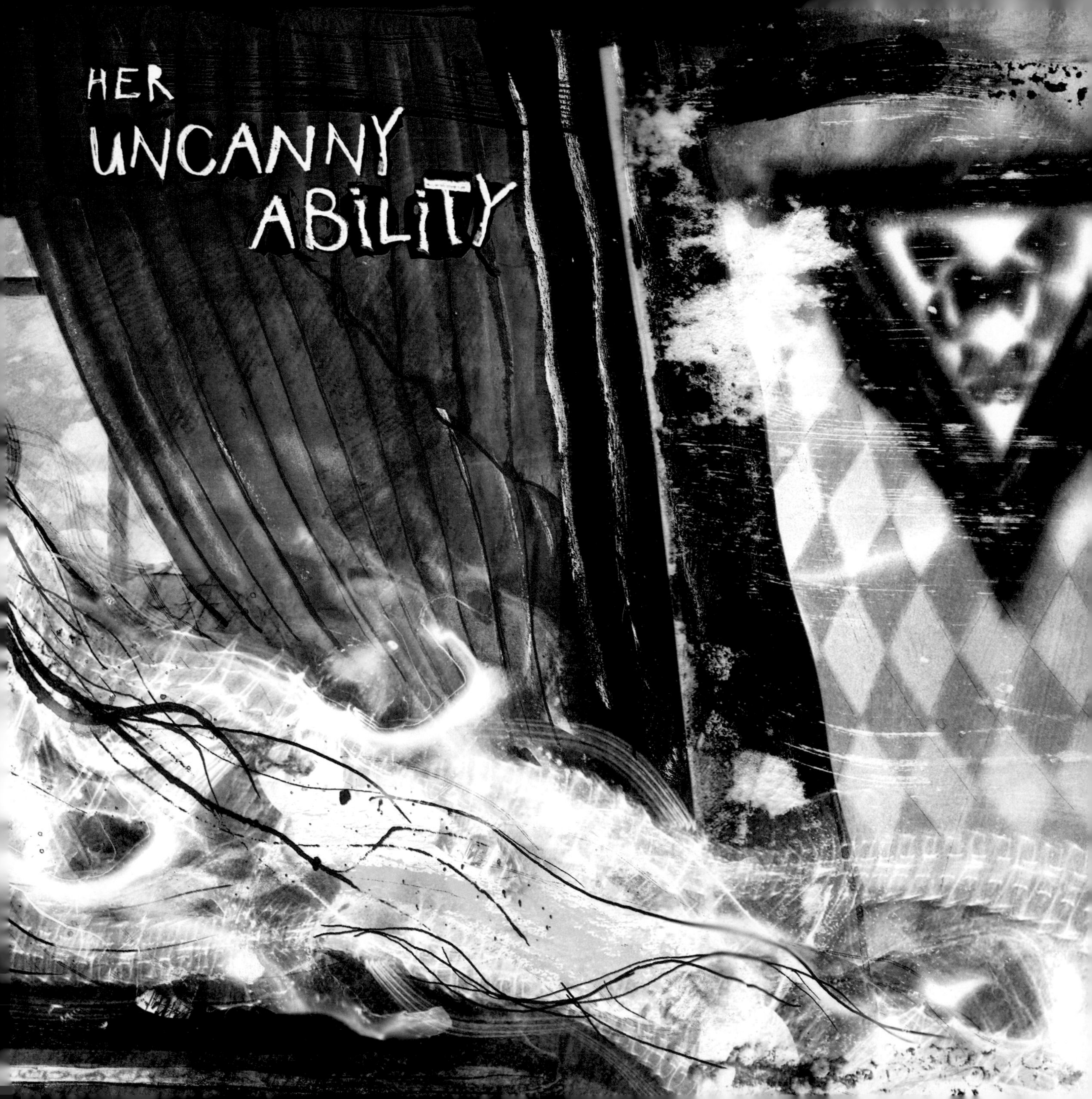
HER
UNCANNY
ABILITY

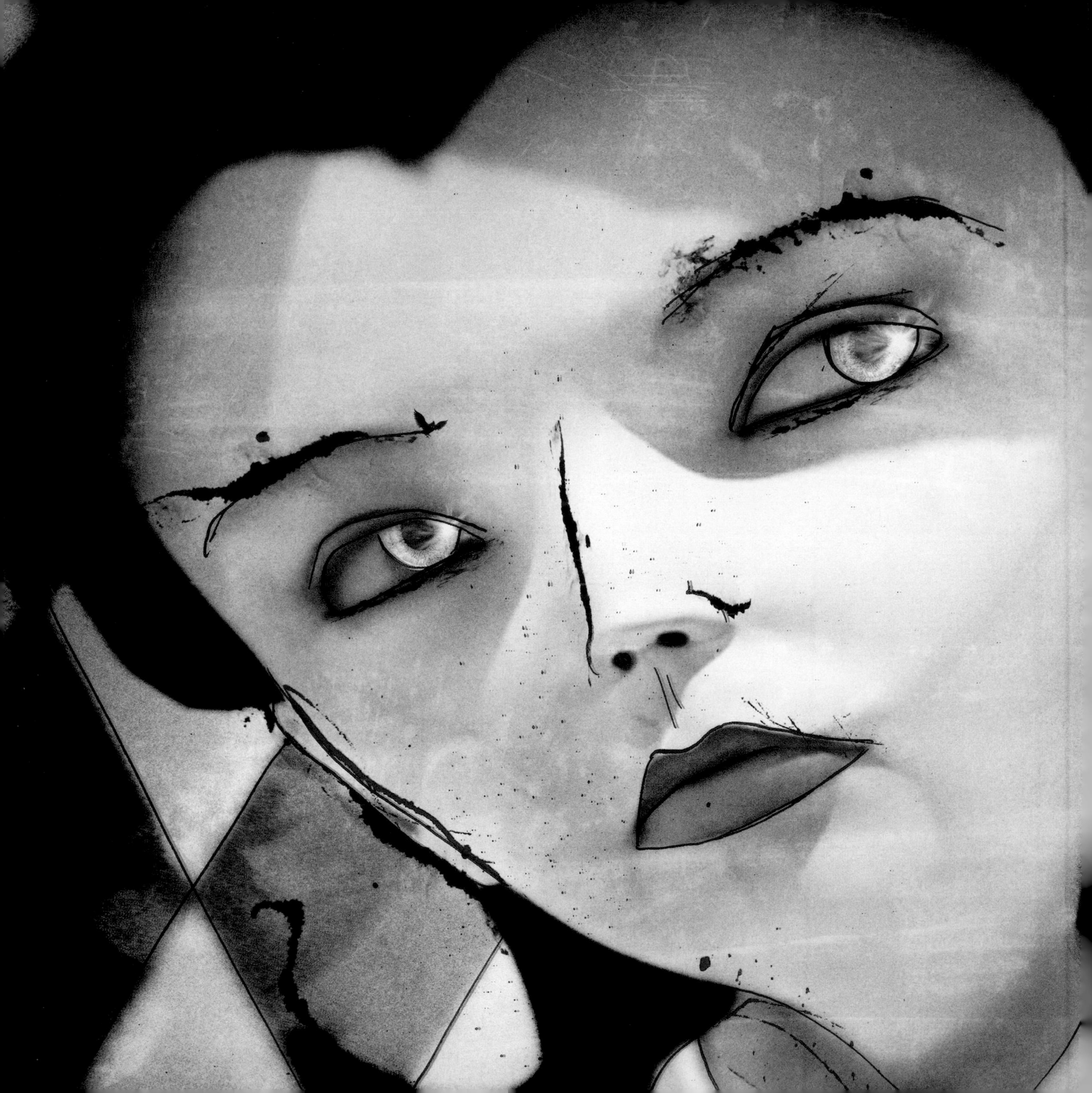

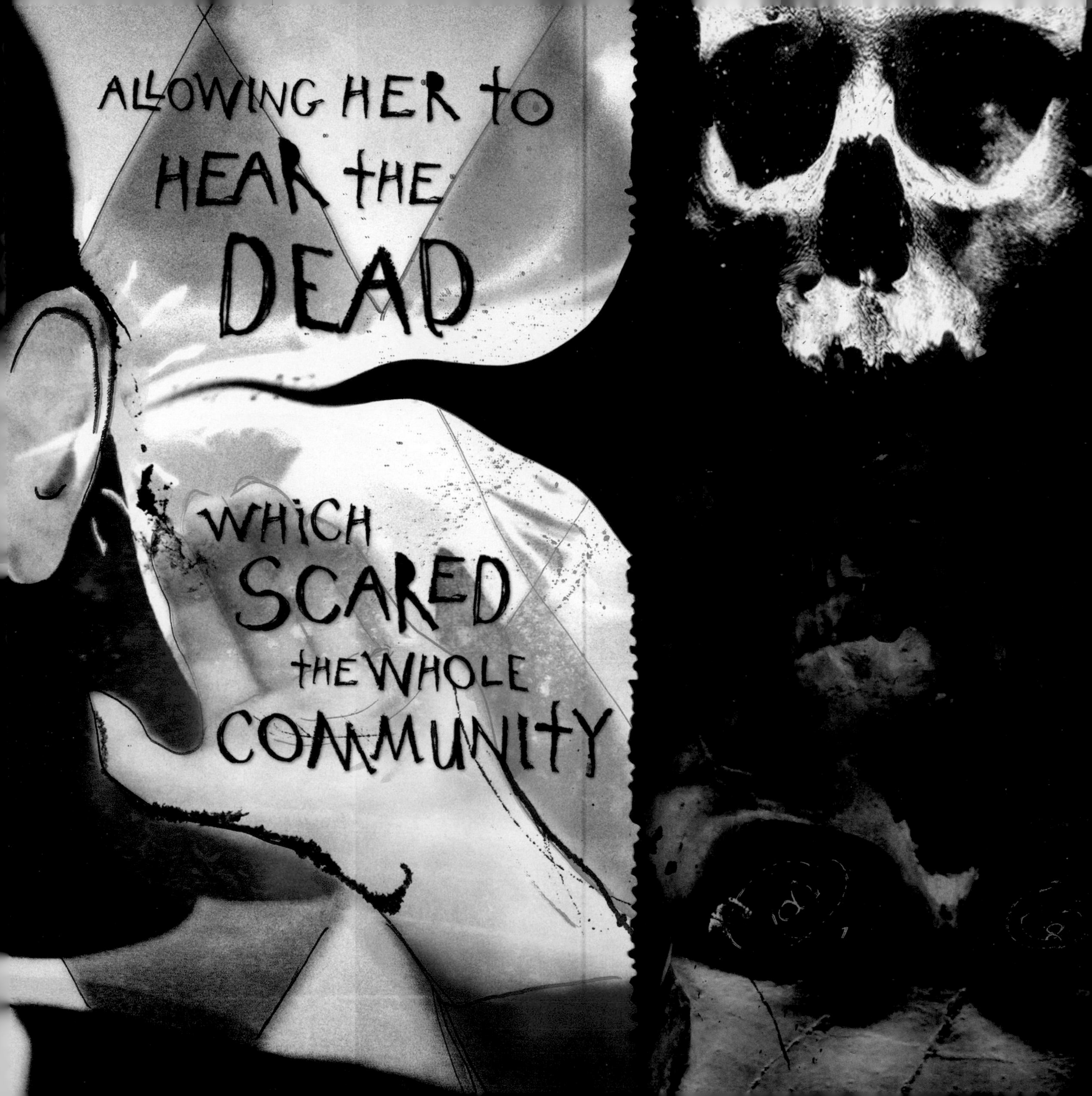
ALLOWING HER TO
HEAR THE
DEAD
WHICH
SCARED
THE WHOLE
COMMUNITY

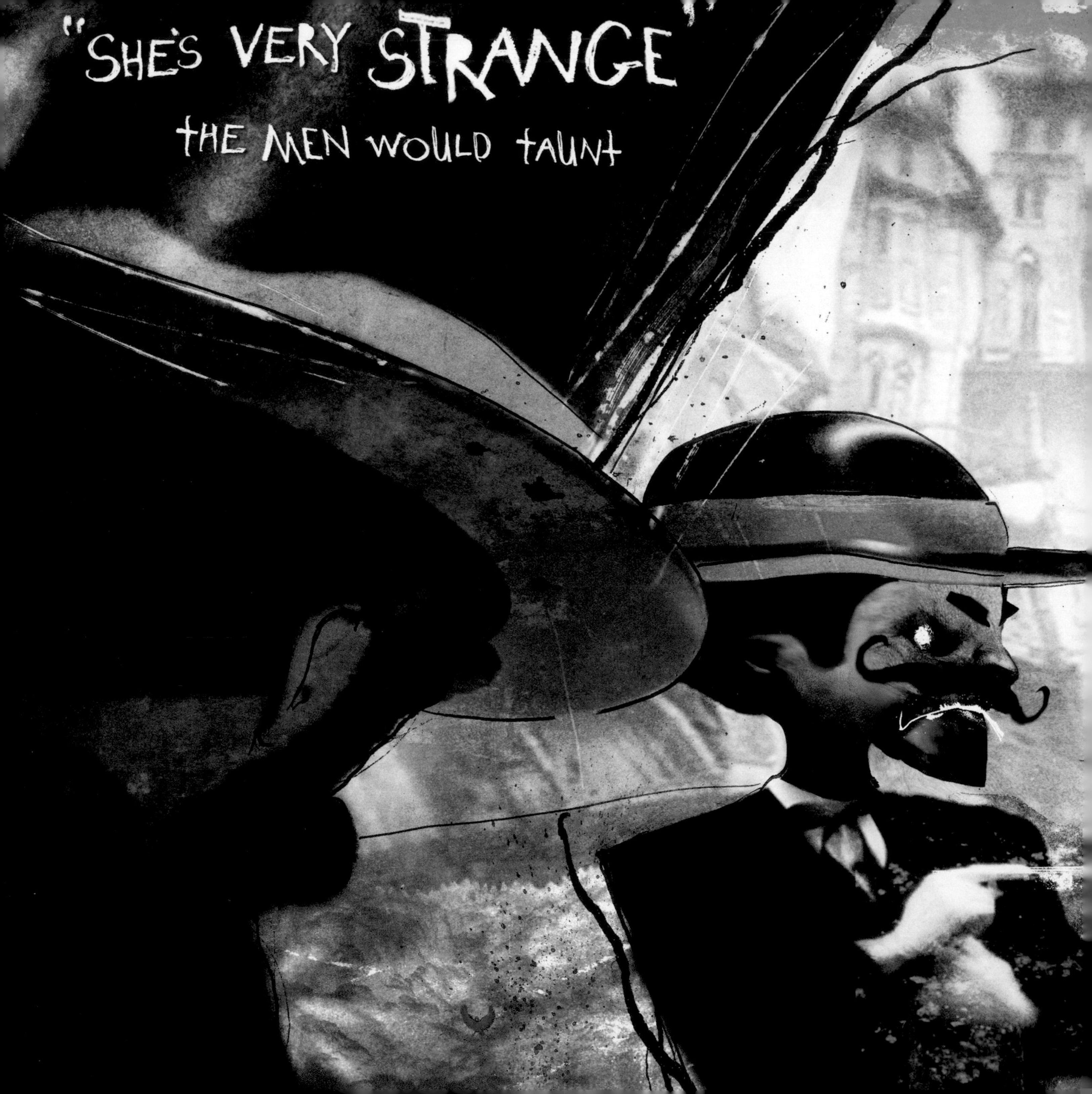
"SHE'S VERY STRANGE"
the MEN WOULD taunt

WHEN SHE'D MAKE A RARE APPEARANCE

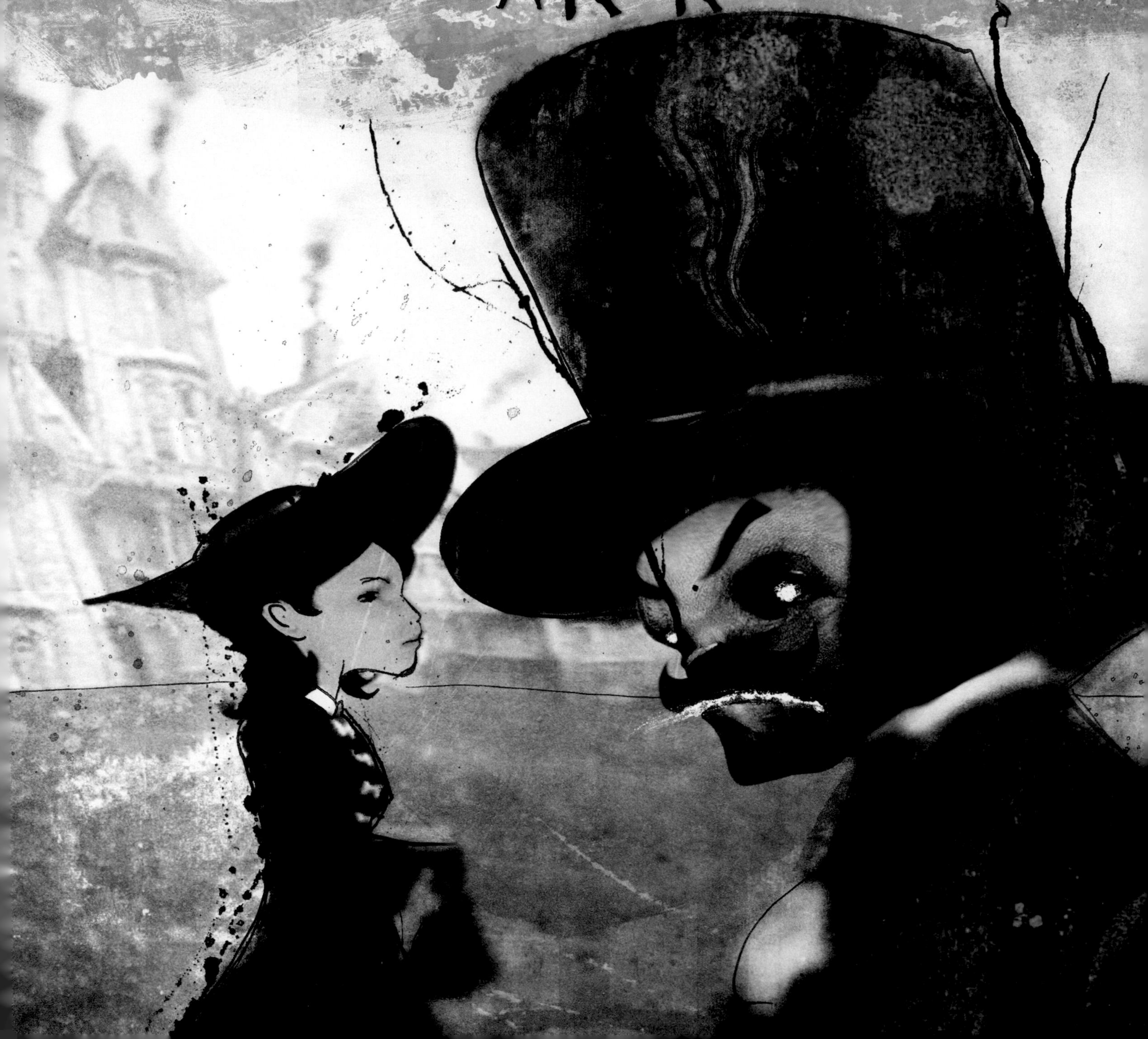

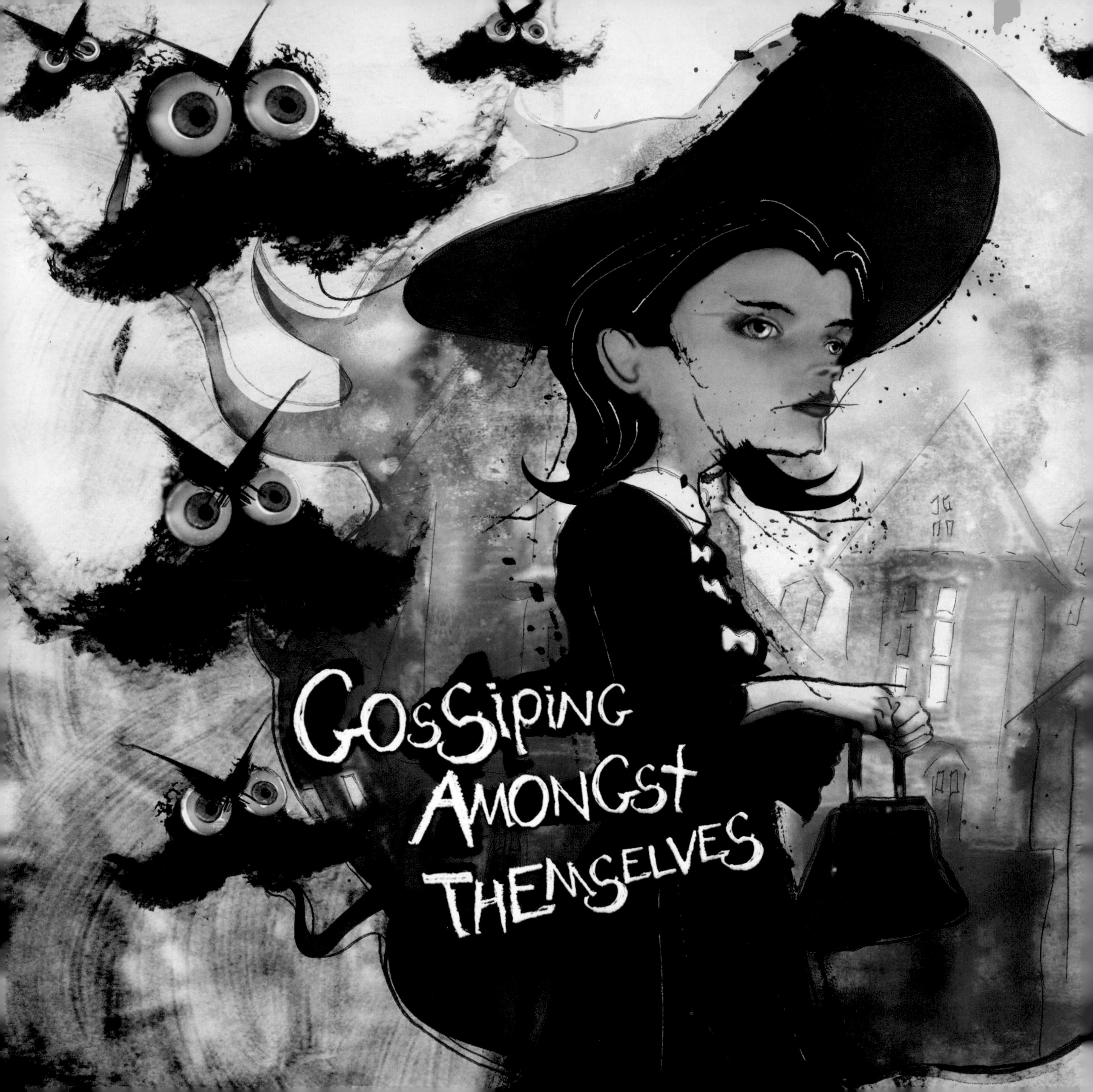
Gossiping
Amongst
Themselves

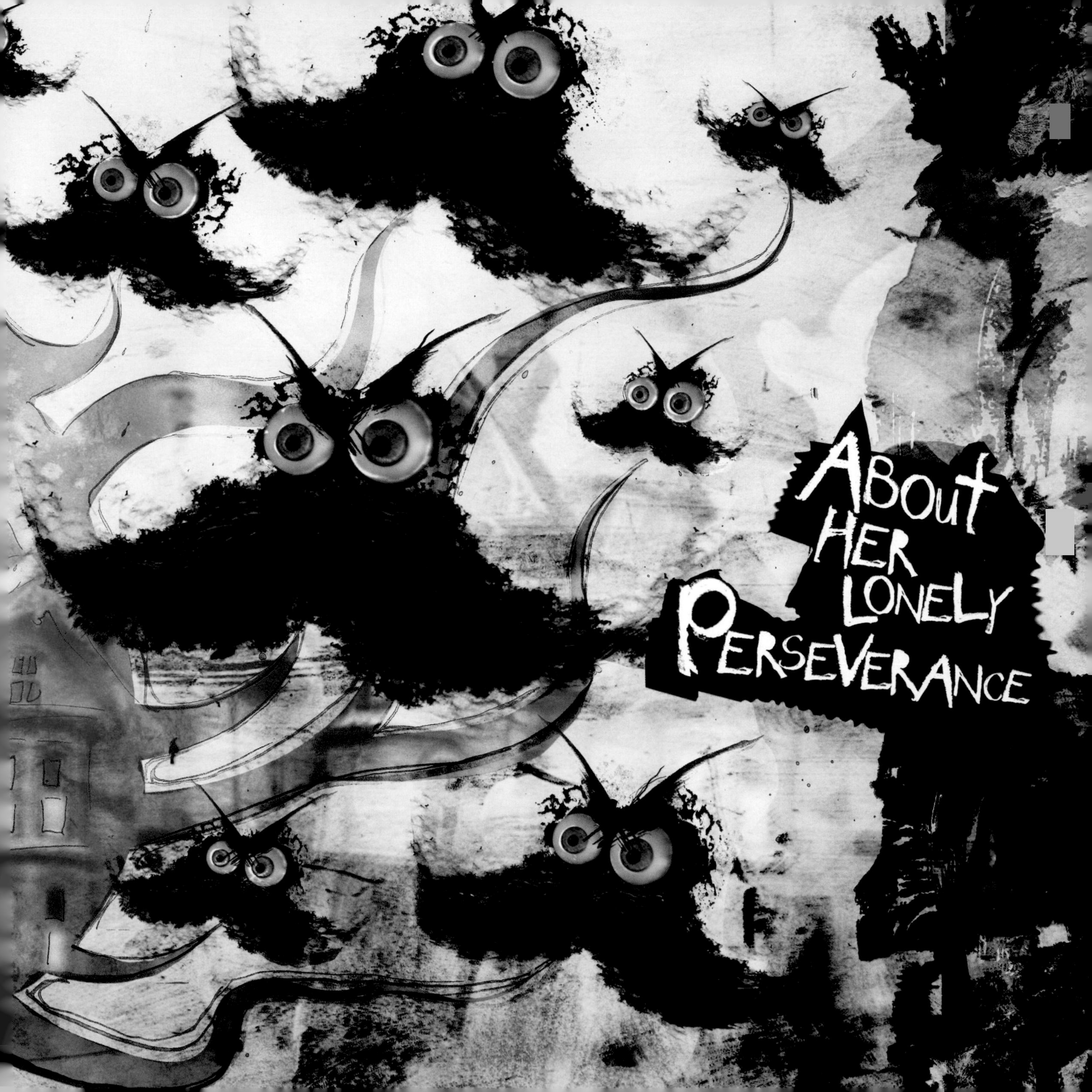
About
Her
Lonely
Perseverance

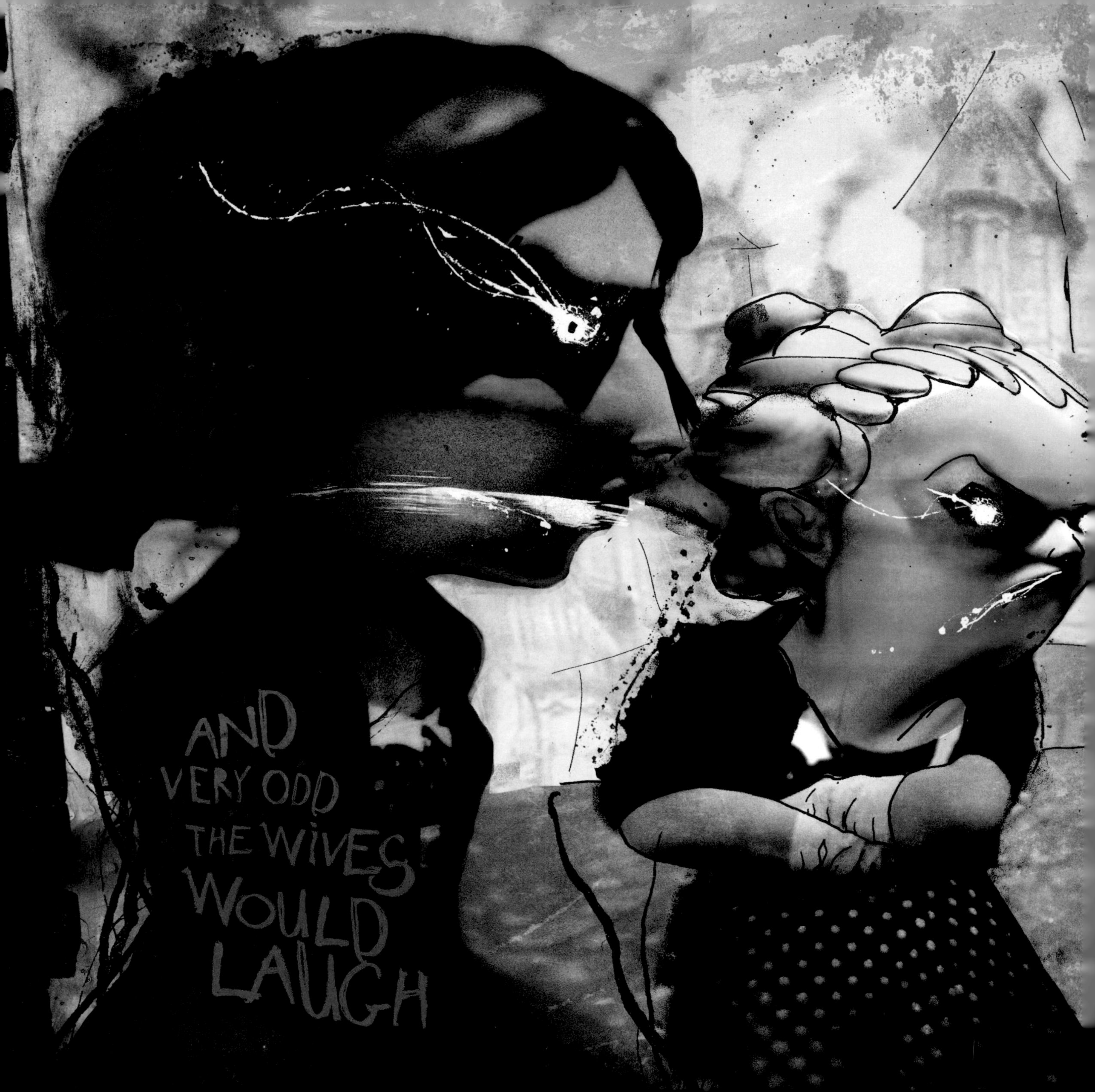
AND
VERY ODD
THE WIVES
WOULD
LAUGH

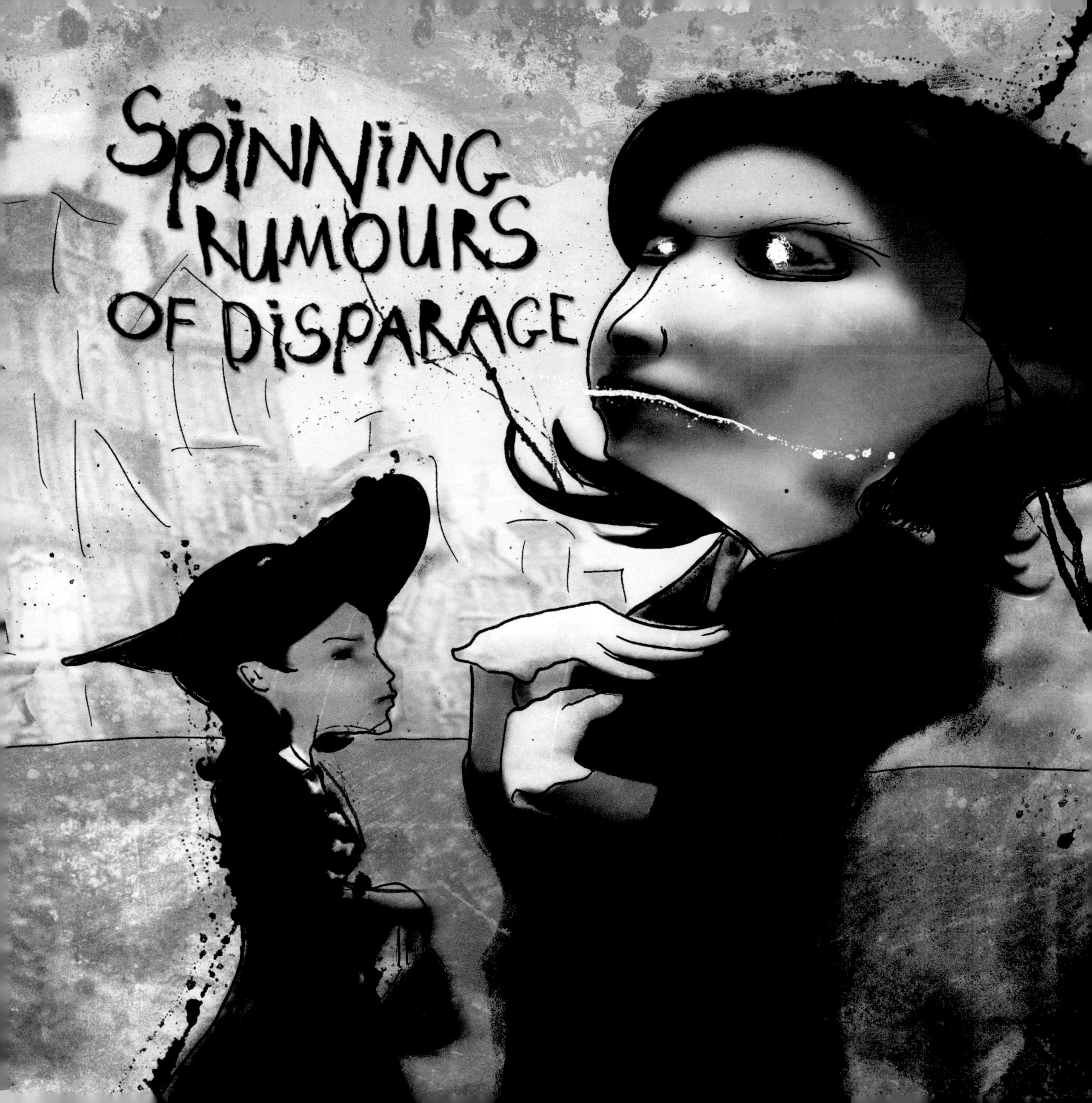
SPINNING RUMOURS OF DISPARAGE

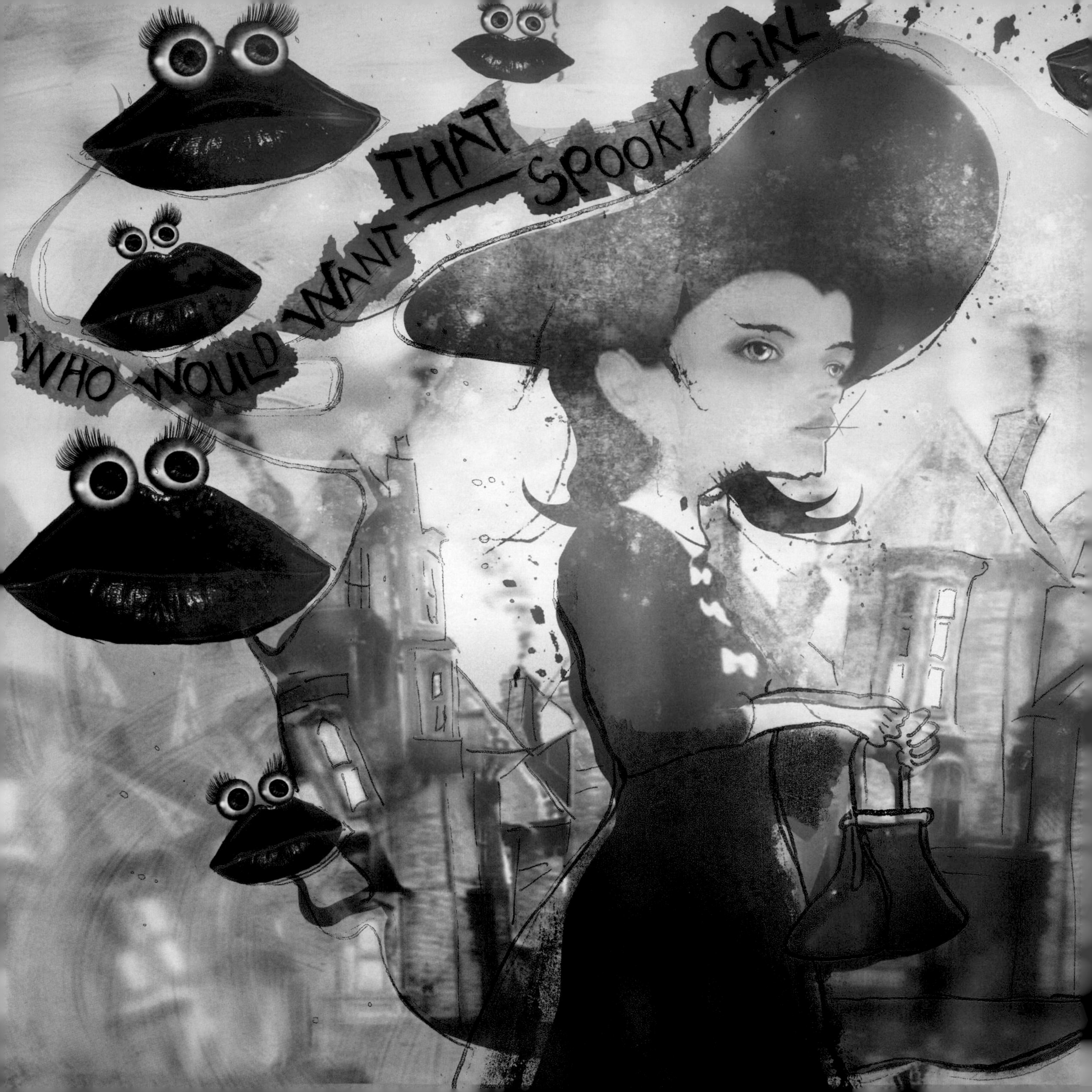
"WHO WOULD WANT THAT SPOOKY GIRL

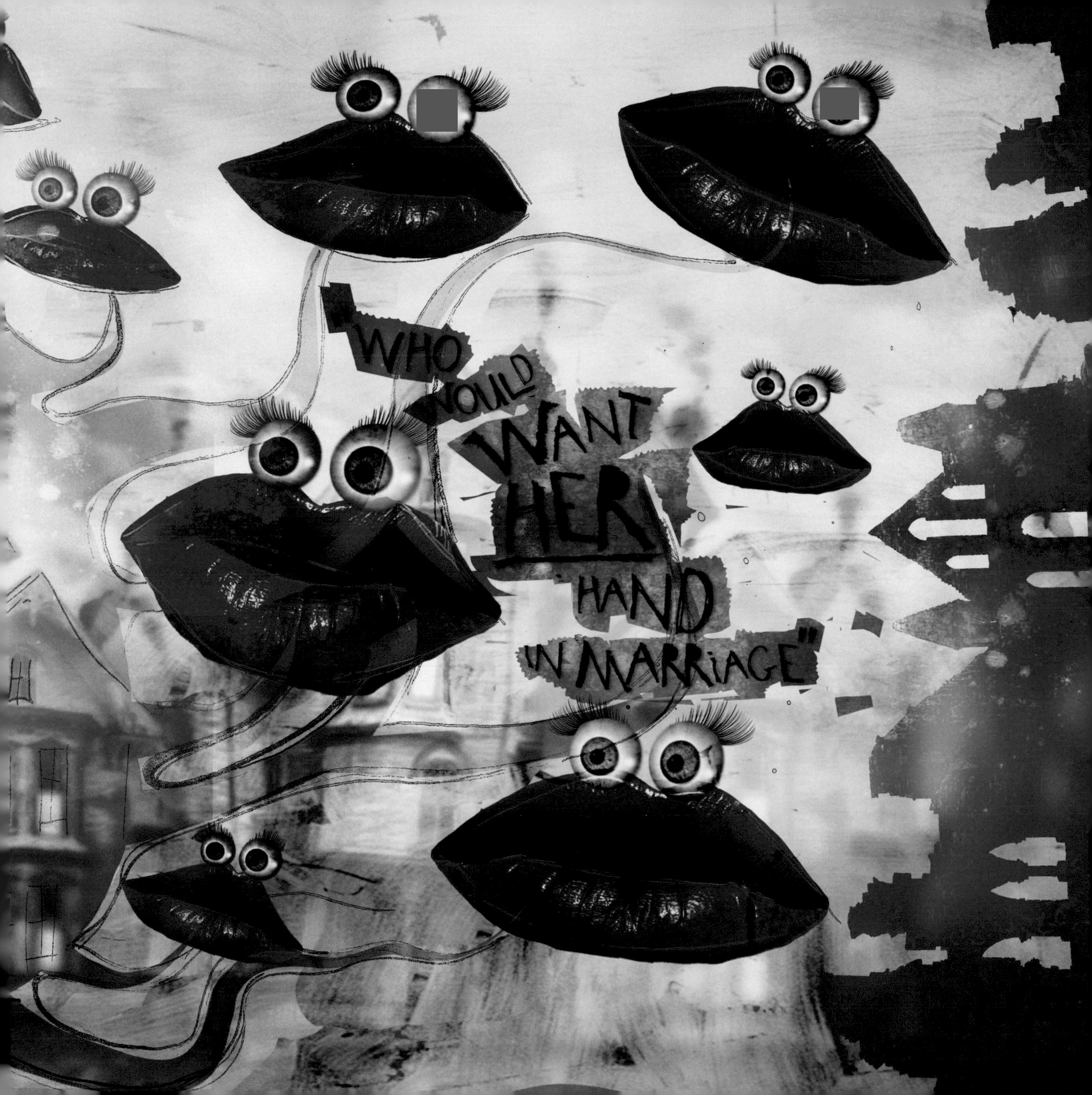
"WHO WOULD WANT HER HAND IN MARRiAGE"

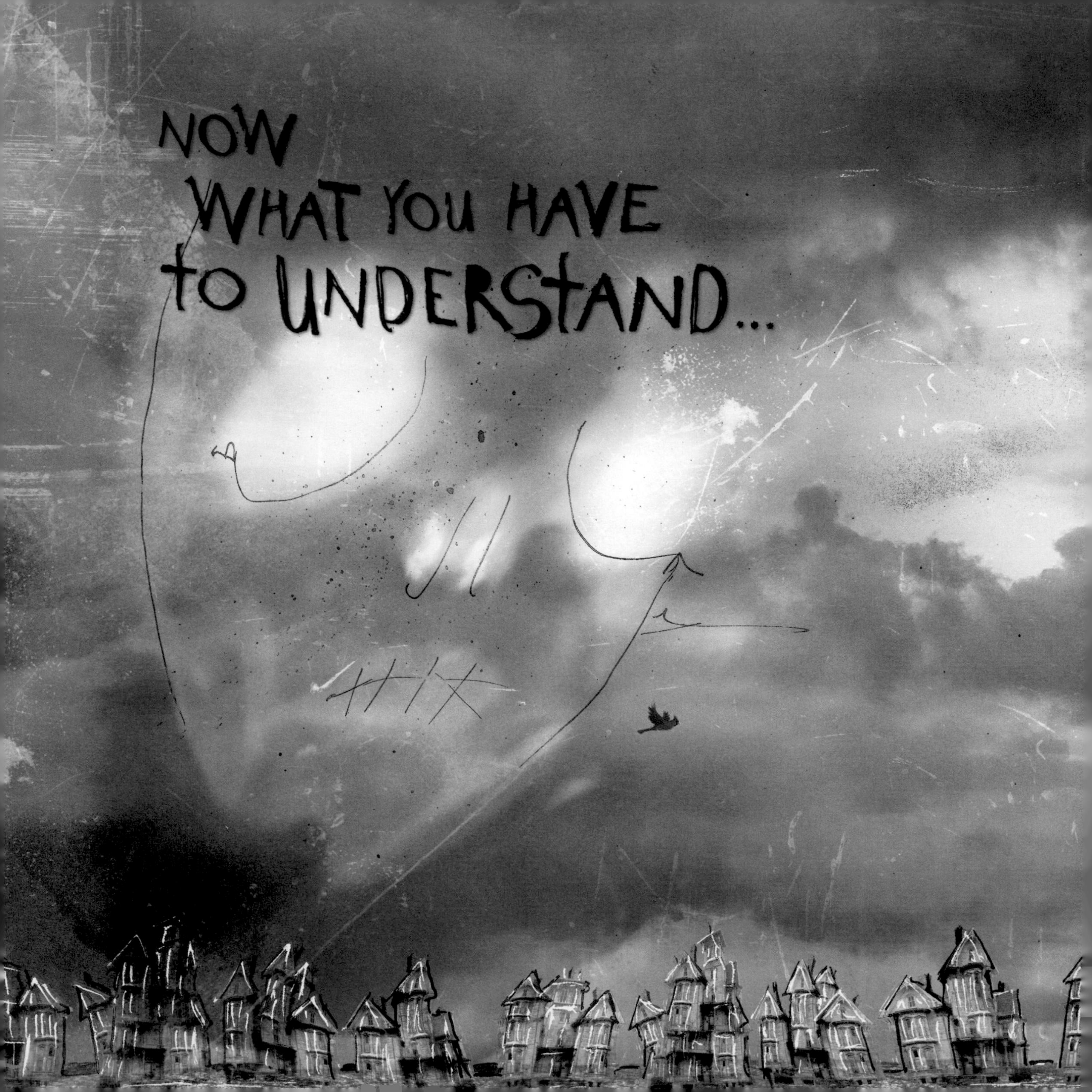
NOW
WHAT YOU HAVE
to UNDERStAND...

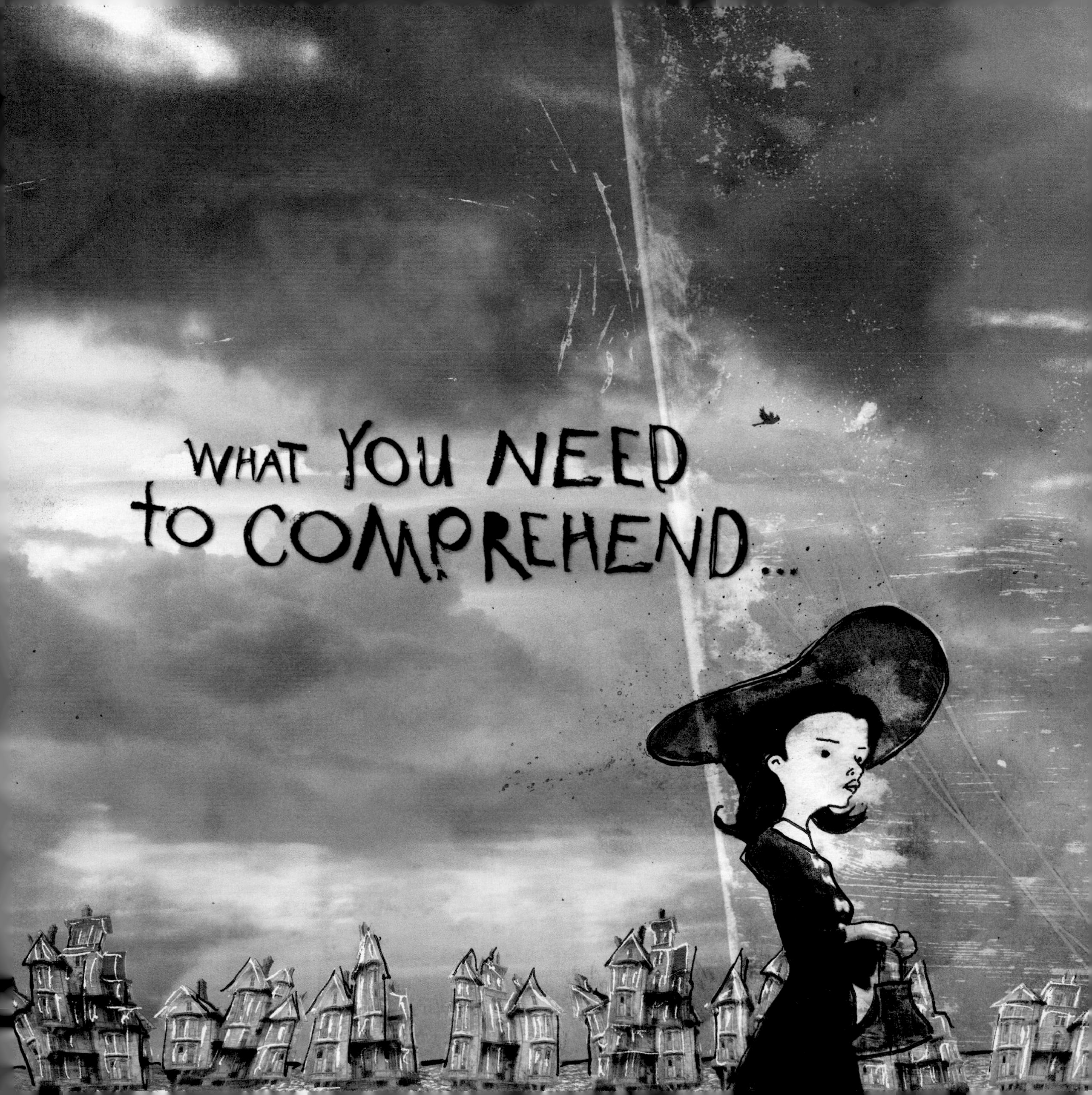
WHAT YOU NEED
to COMPREHEND...

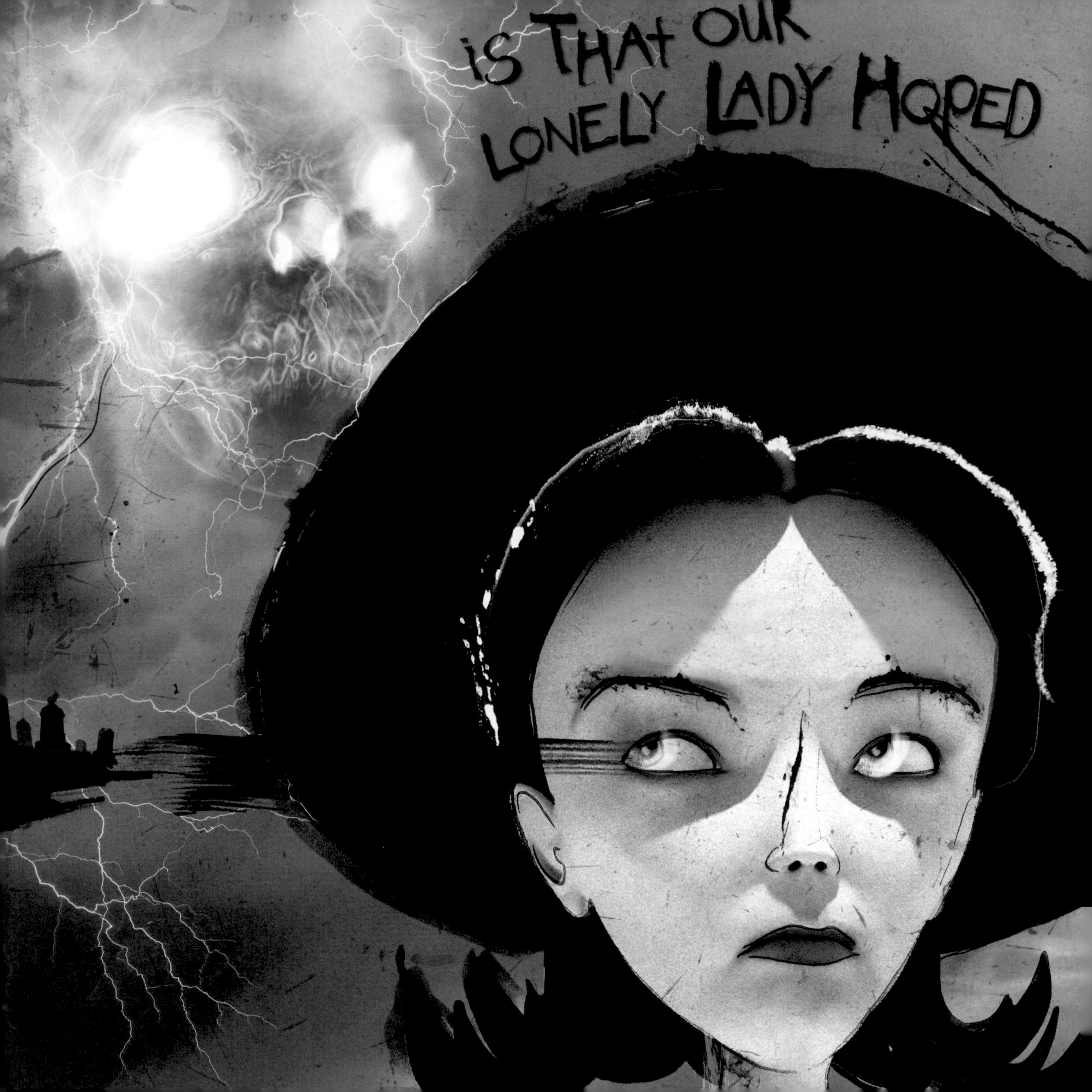
is That our
Lonely Lady Hoped

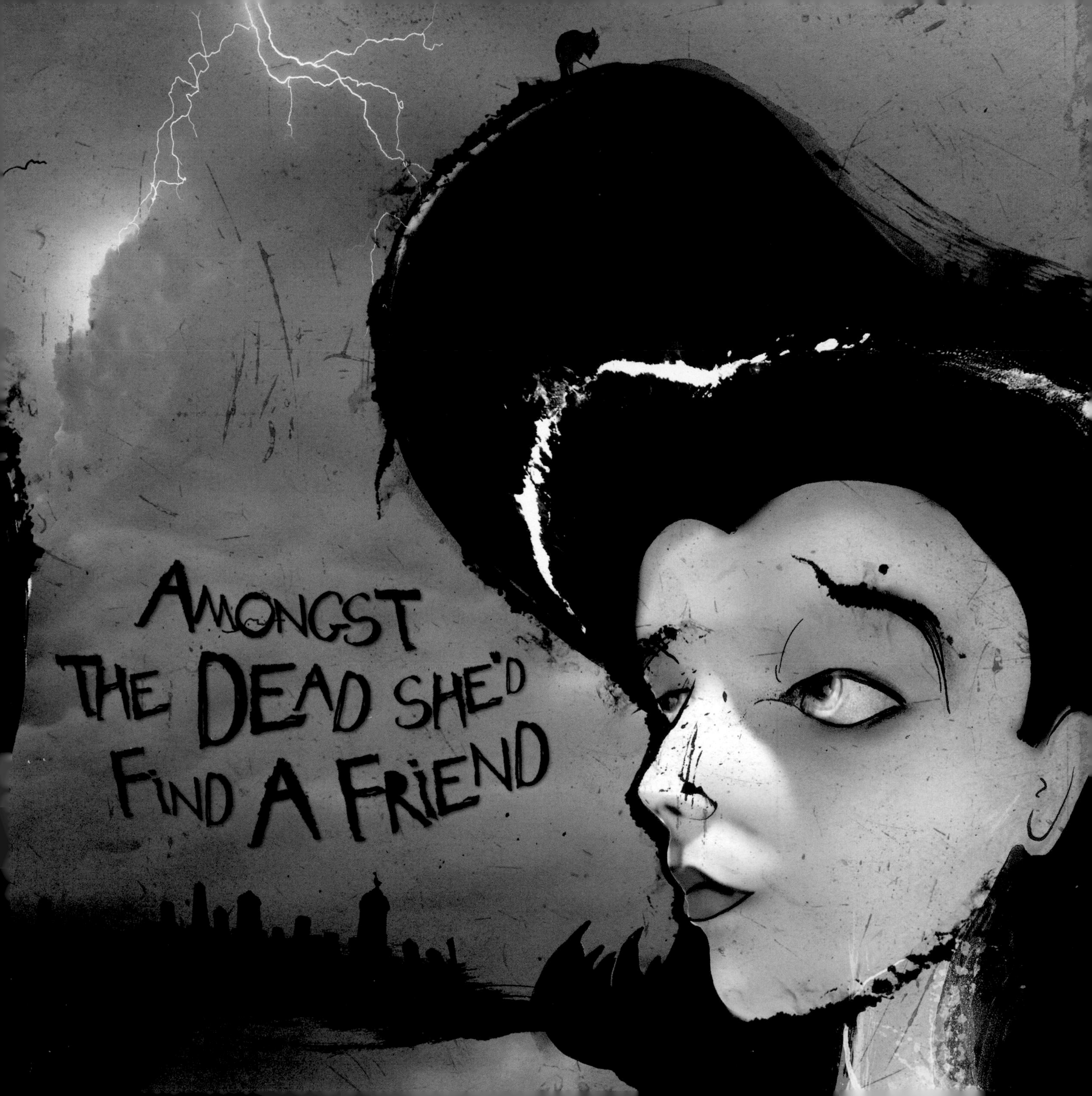
AMONGST
THE DEAD SHE'D
FIND A FRIEND

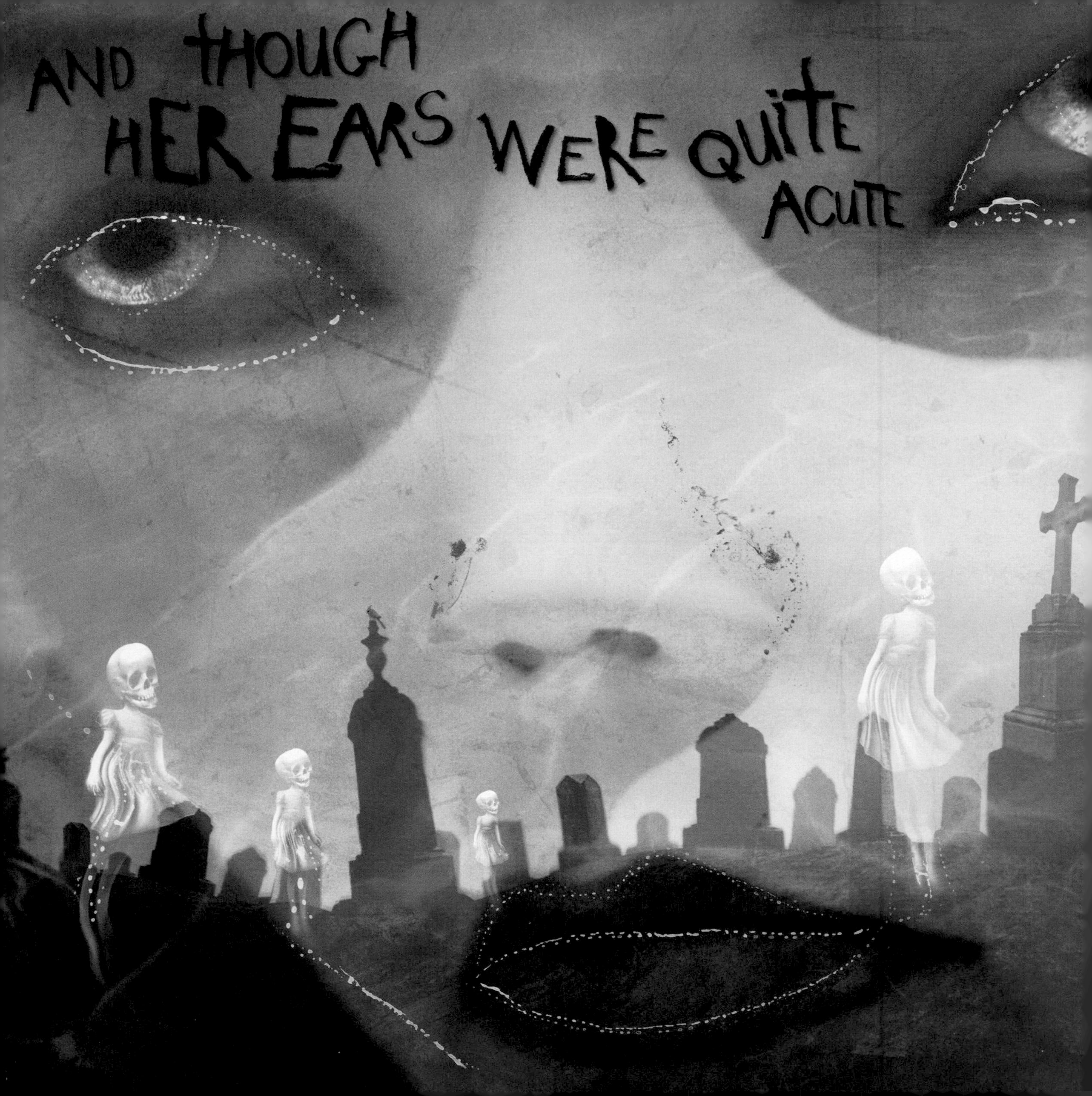
AND THOUGH
HER EARS WERE QUITE
ACUTE

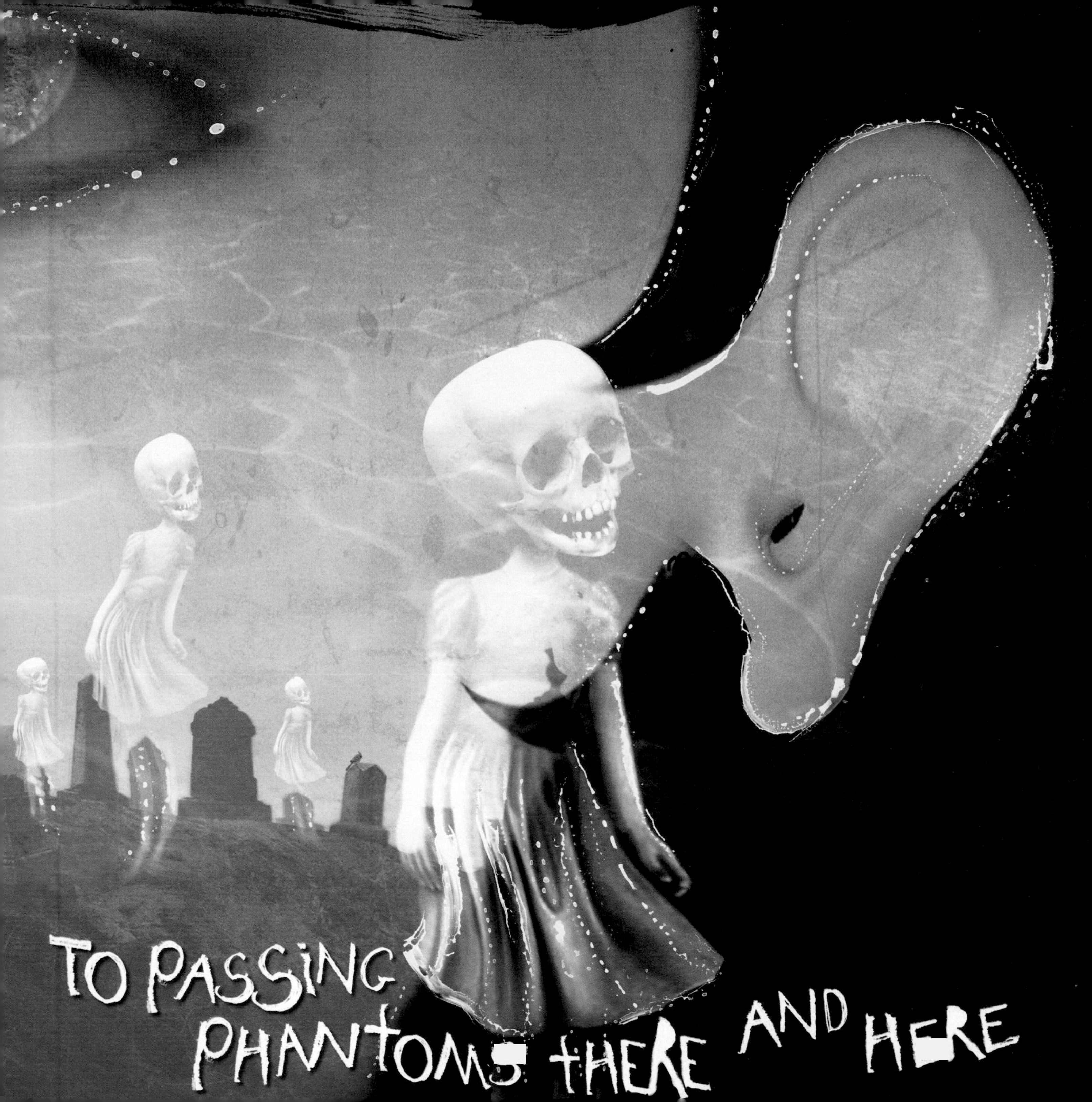
TO PASSING
PHANTOMS THERE AND HERE

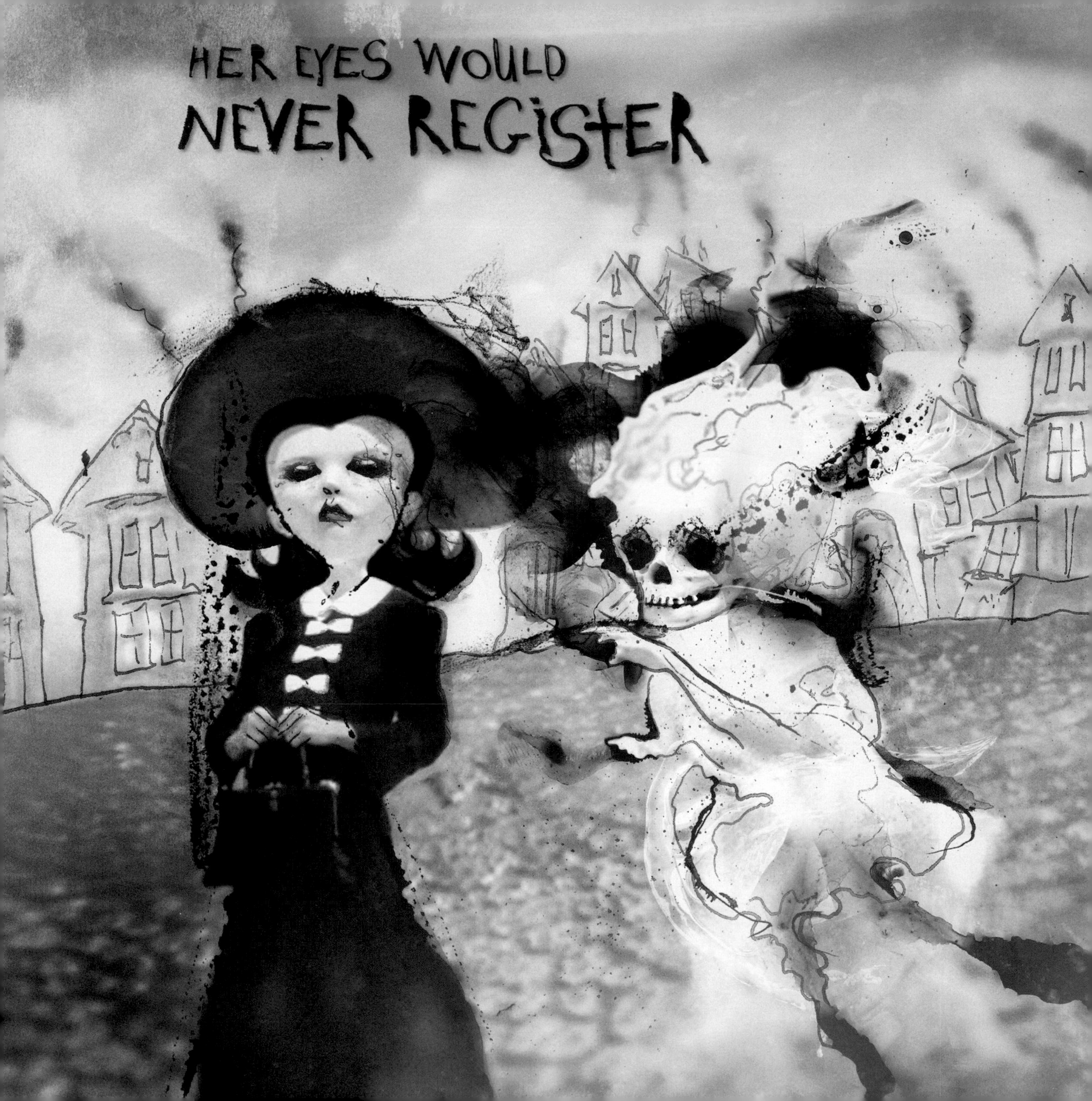
HER EYES WOULD
NEVER REGISTER

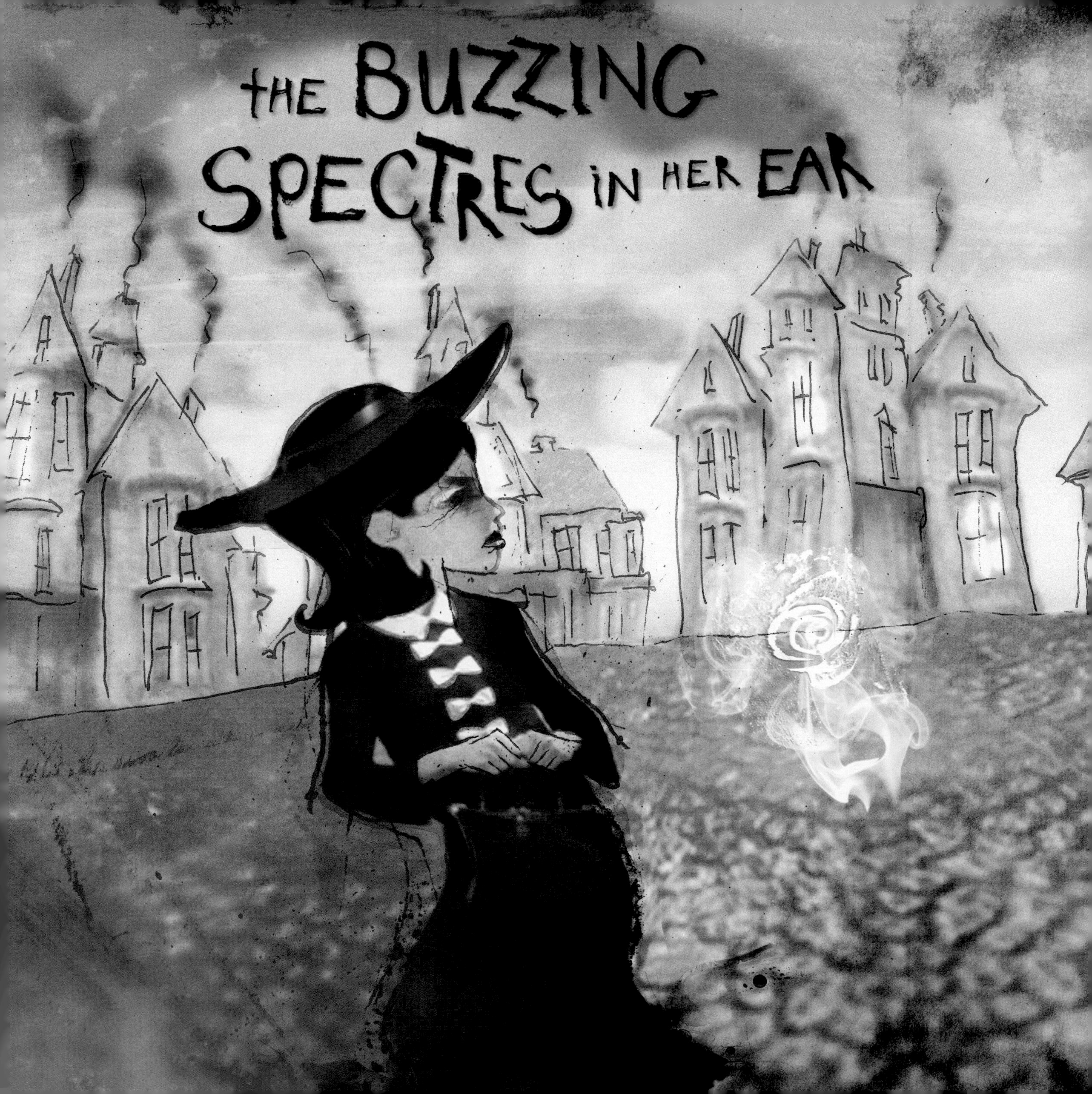
the BUZZING
SPECTRES IN HER EAR

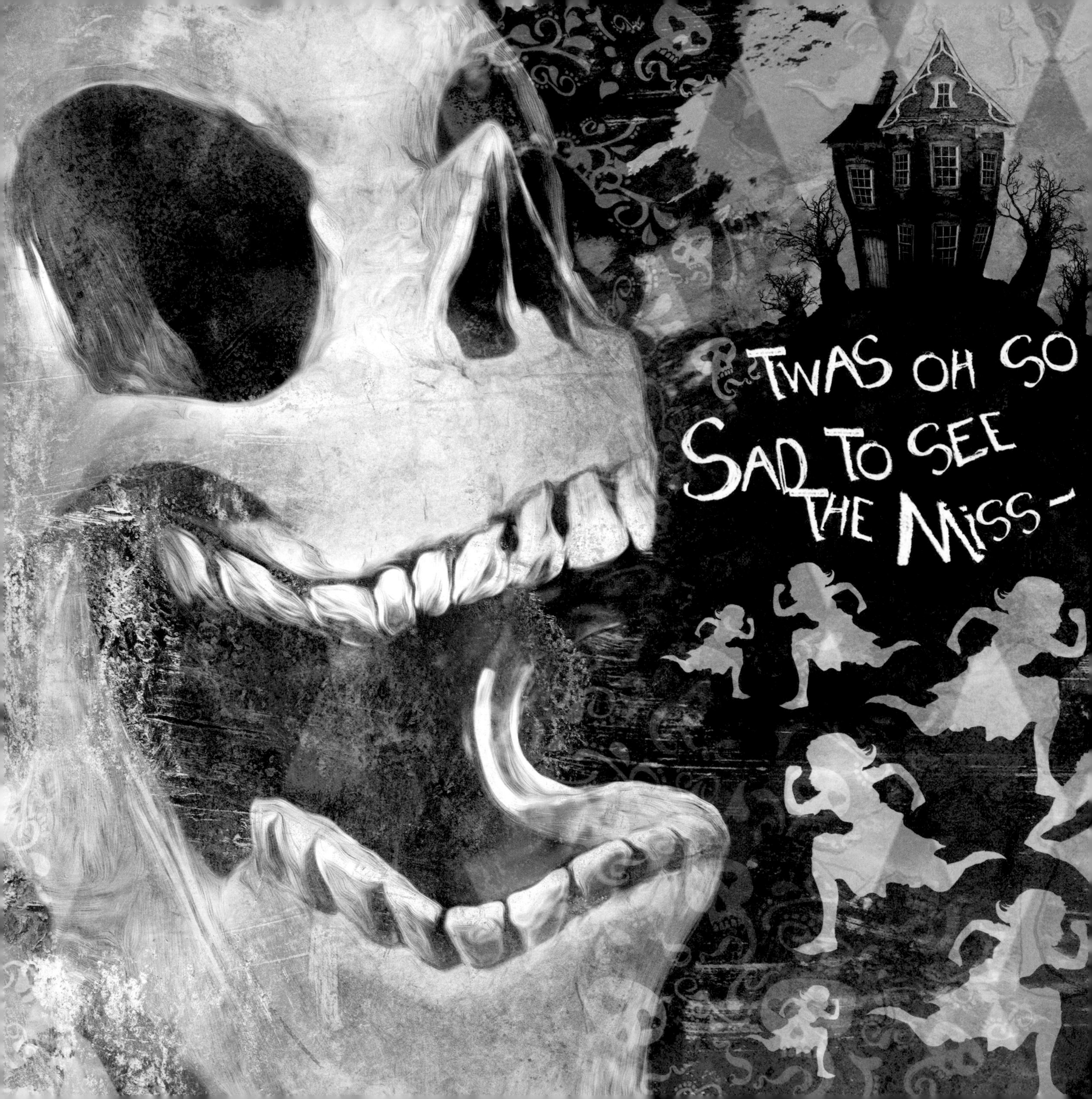
TWAS OH SO
SAD TO SEE
THE MISS -

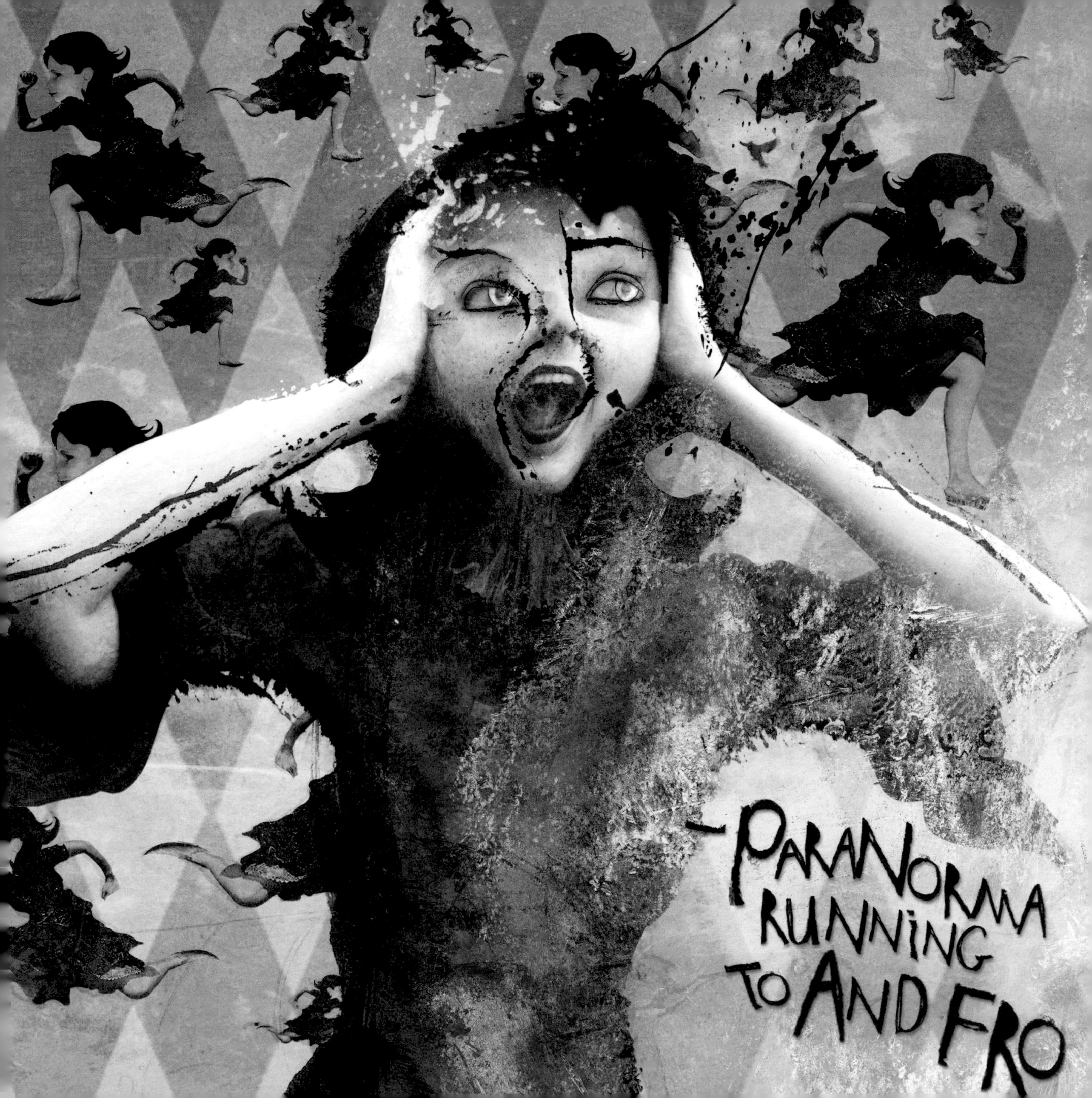
PARANORMA
RUNNING
TO AND FRO

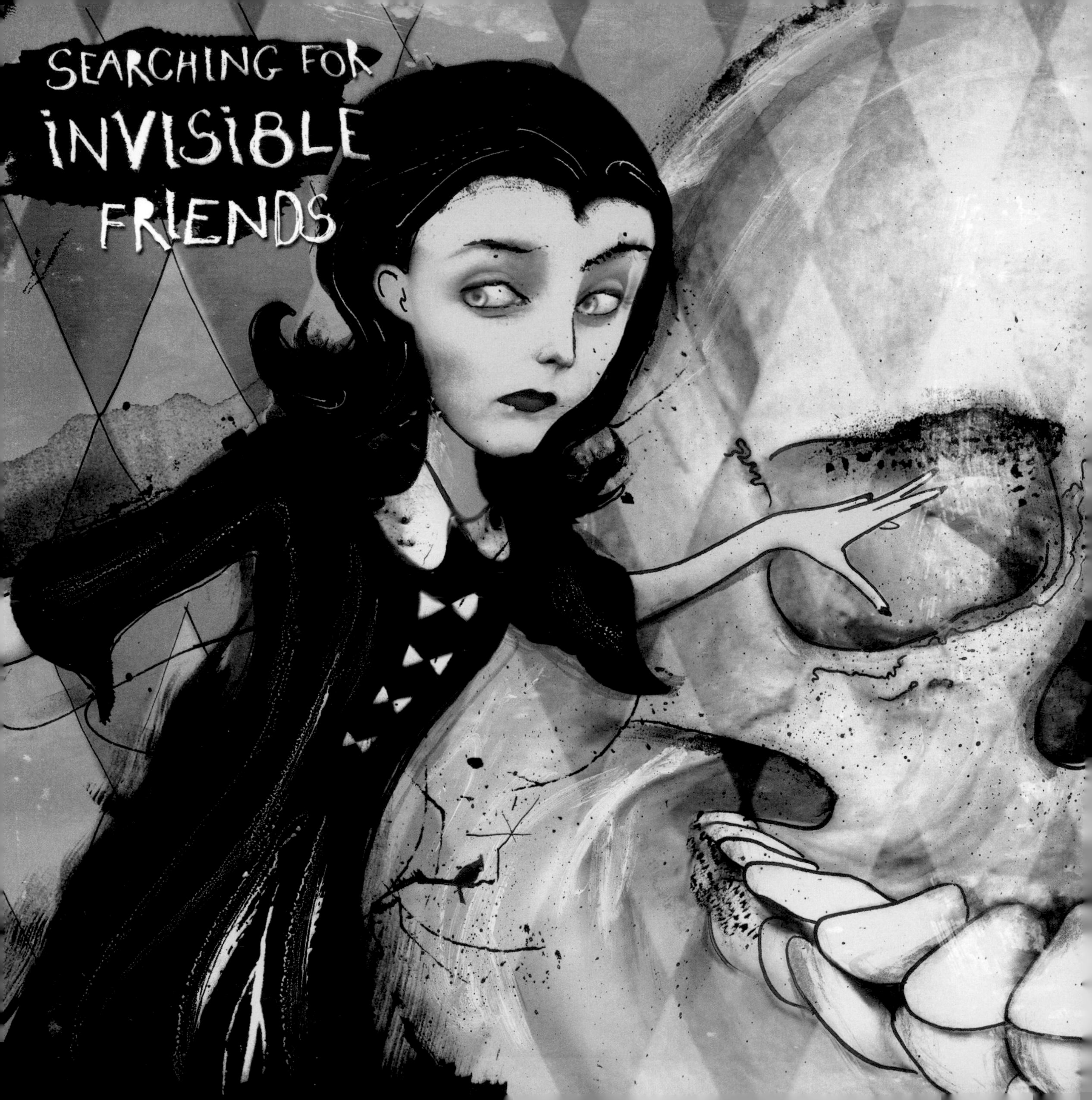
SEARCHING FOR
INVISIBLE
FRIENDS

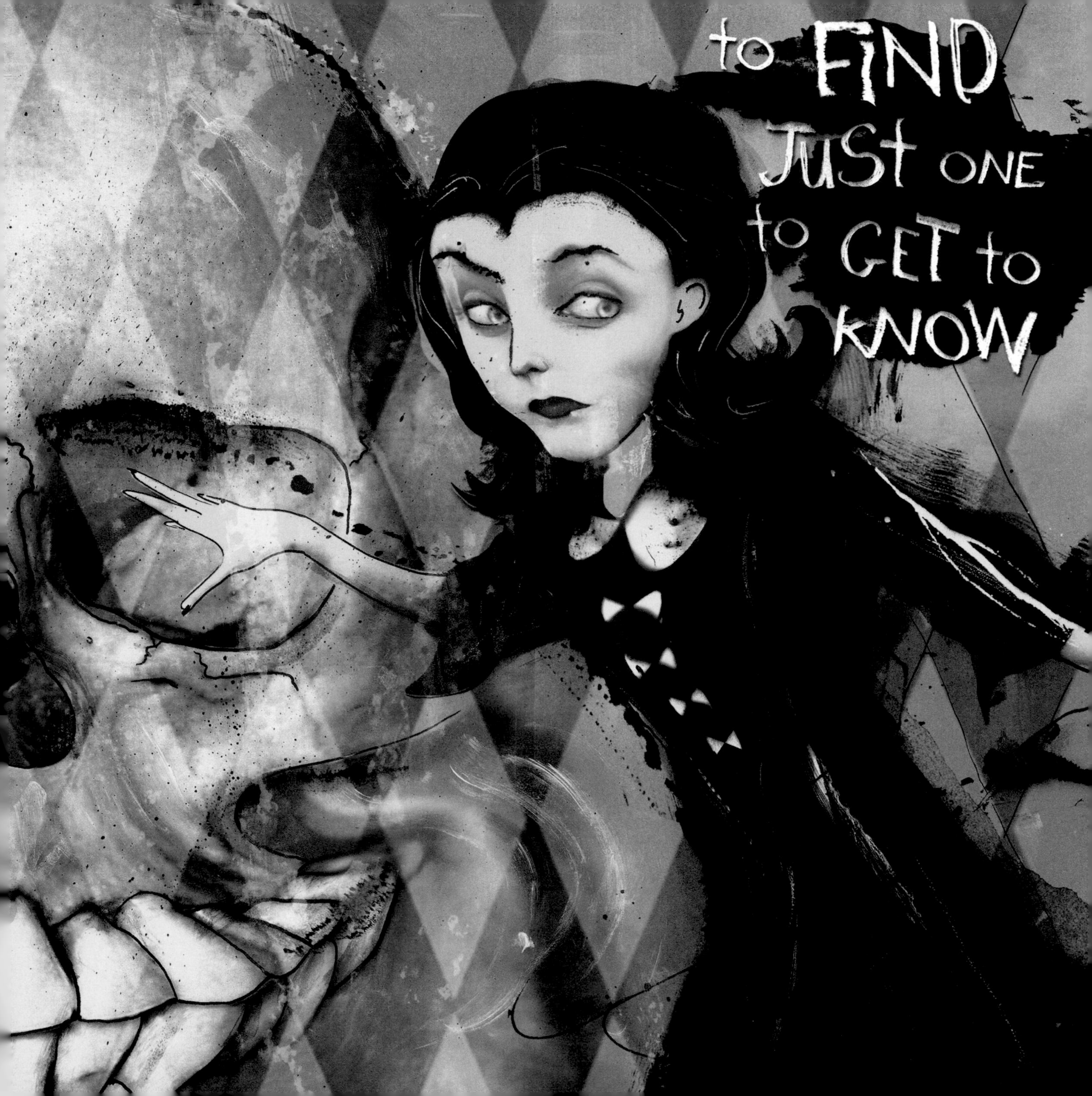
to FIND
JUST ONE
to GET to
KNOW

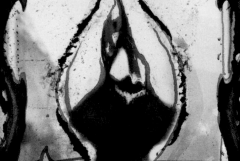

AND THEN ONE DAY
iT BEGAN to END

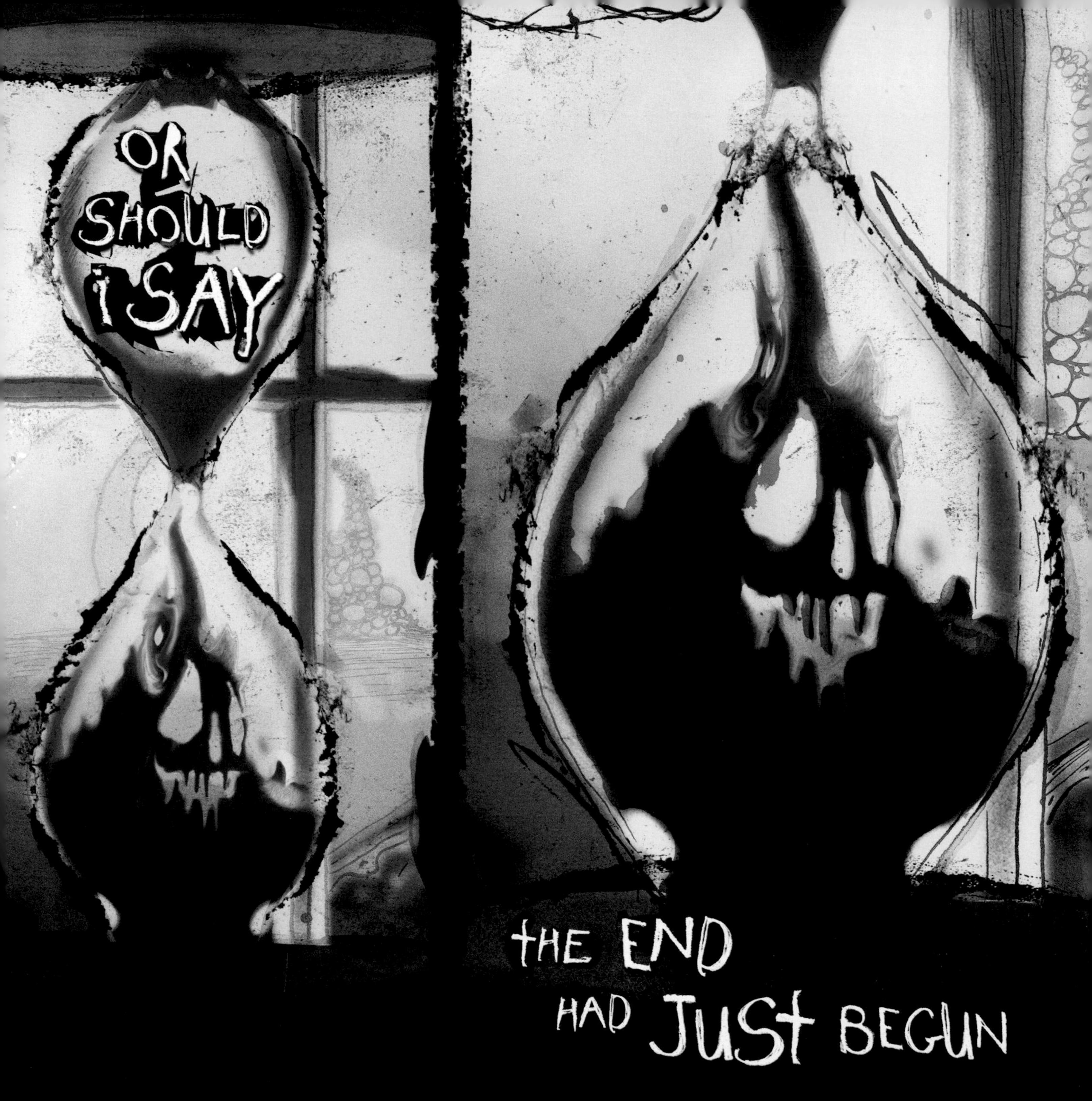
OR SHOULD I SAY
THE END HAD JUST BEGUN

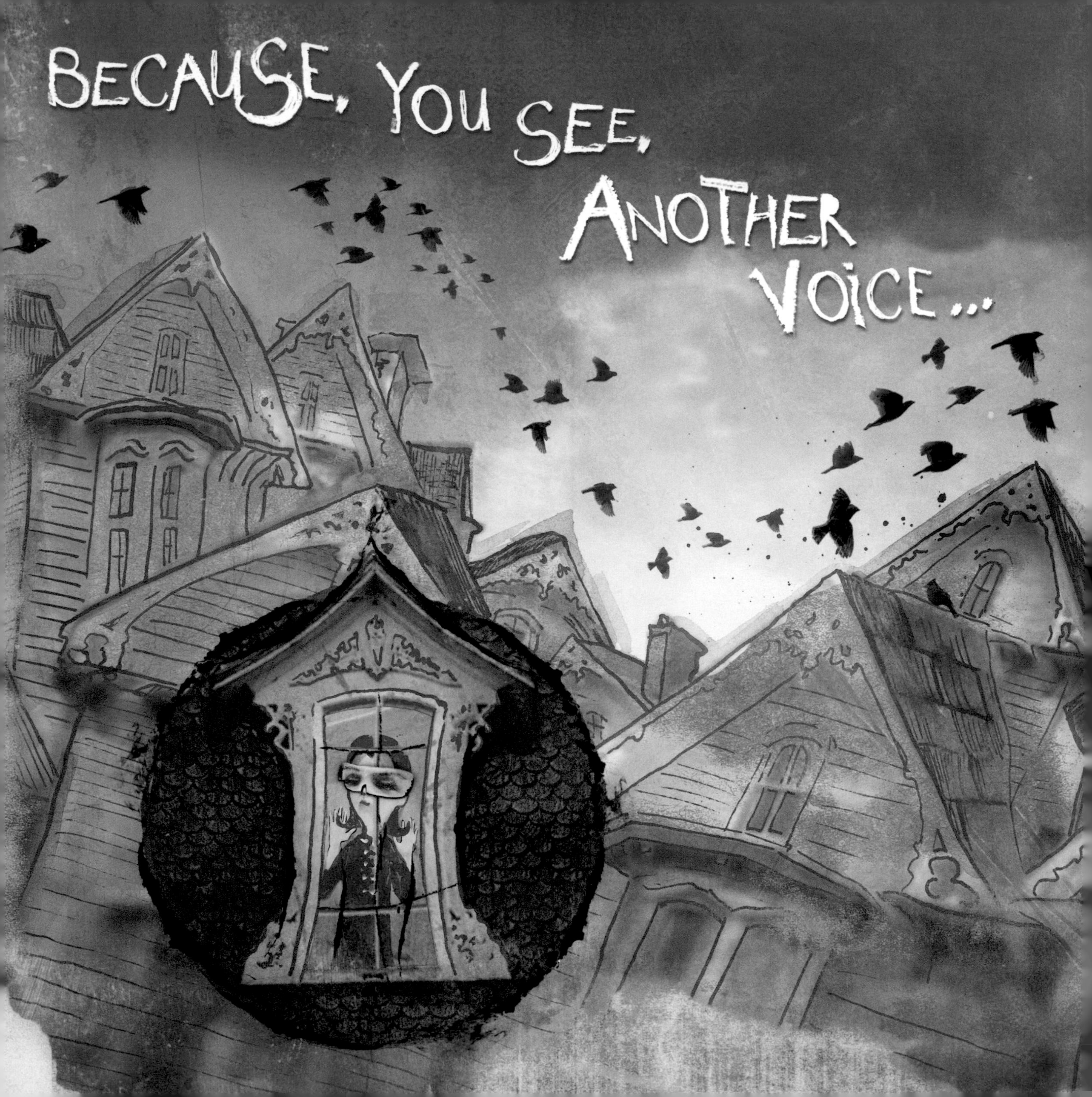
Because, you see, another voice…

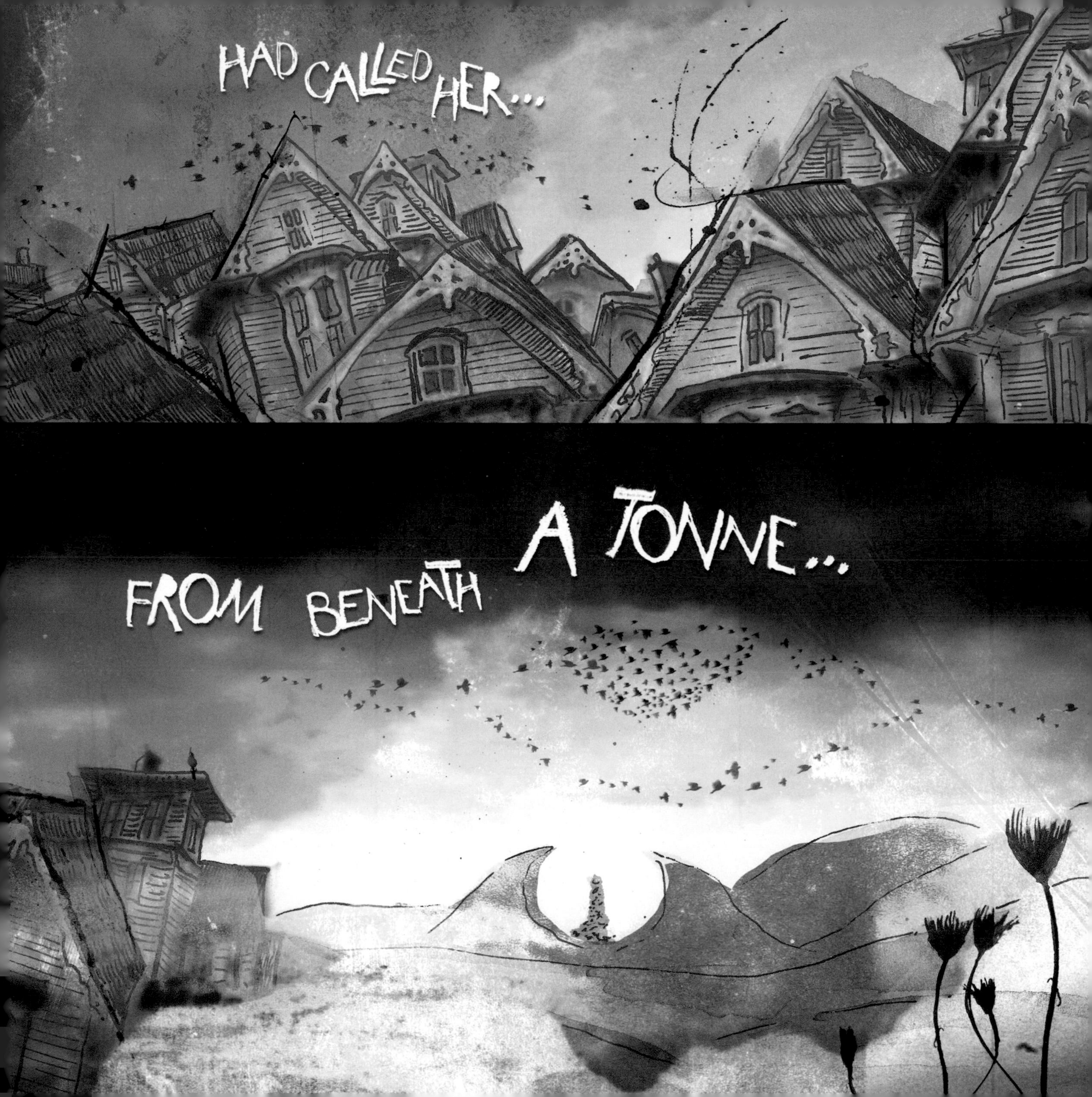
HAD CALLED HER...
FROM BENEATH A TONNE...

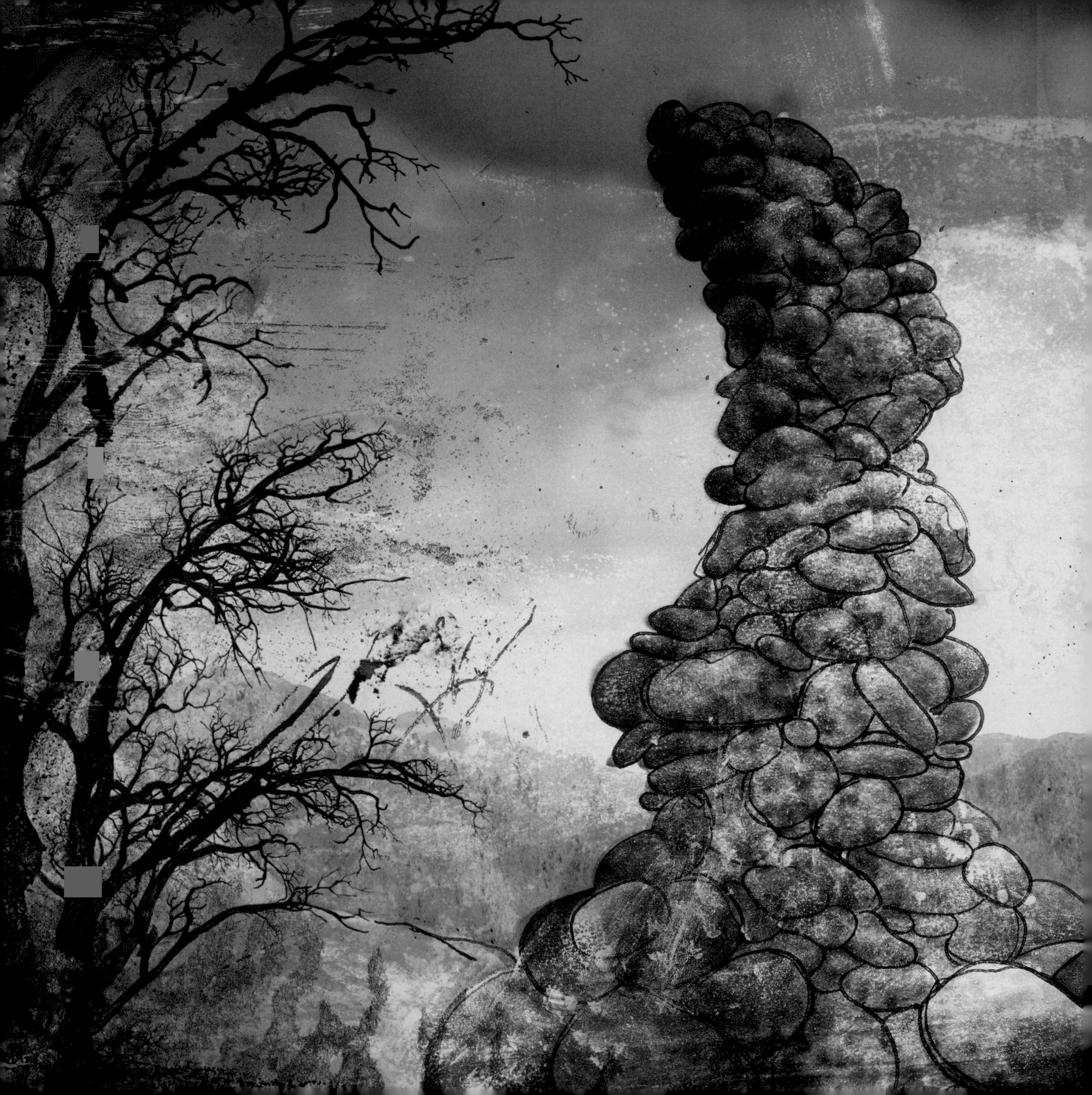

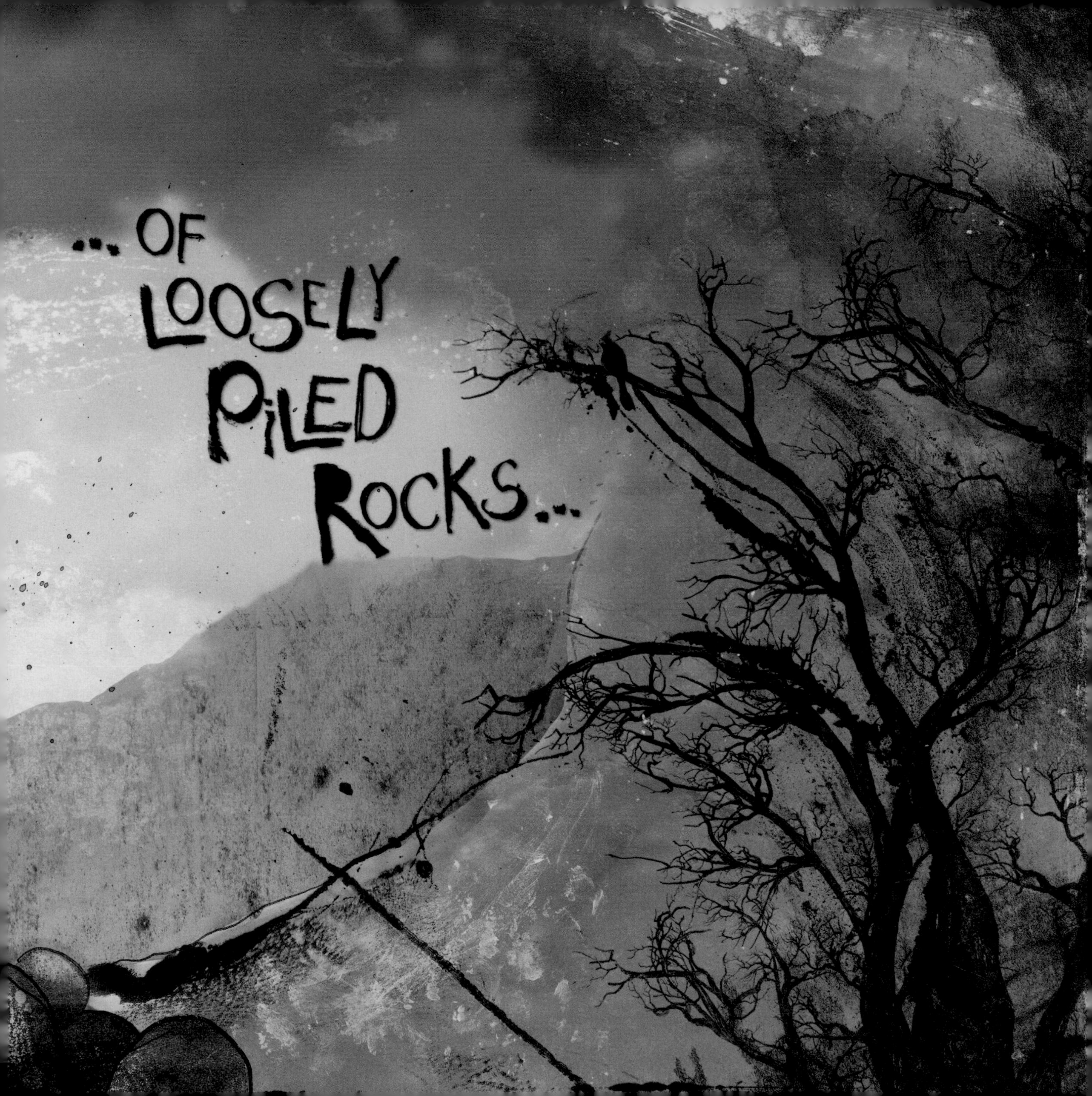
... OF LOOSELY PILED ROCKS ...

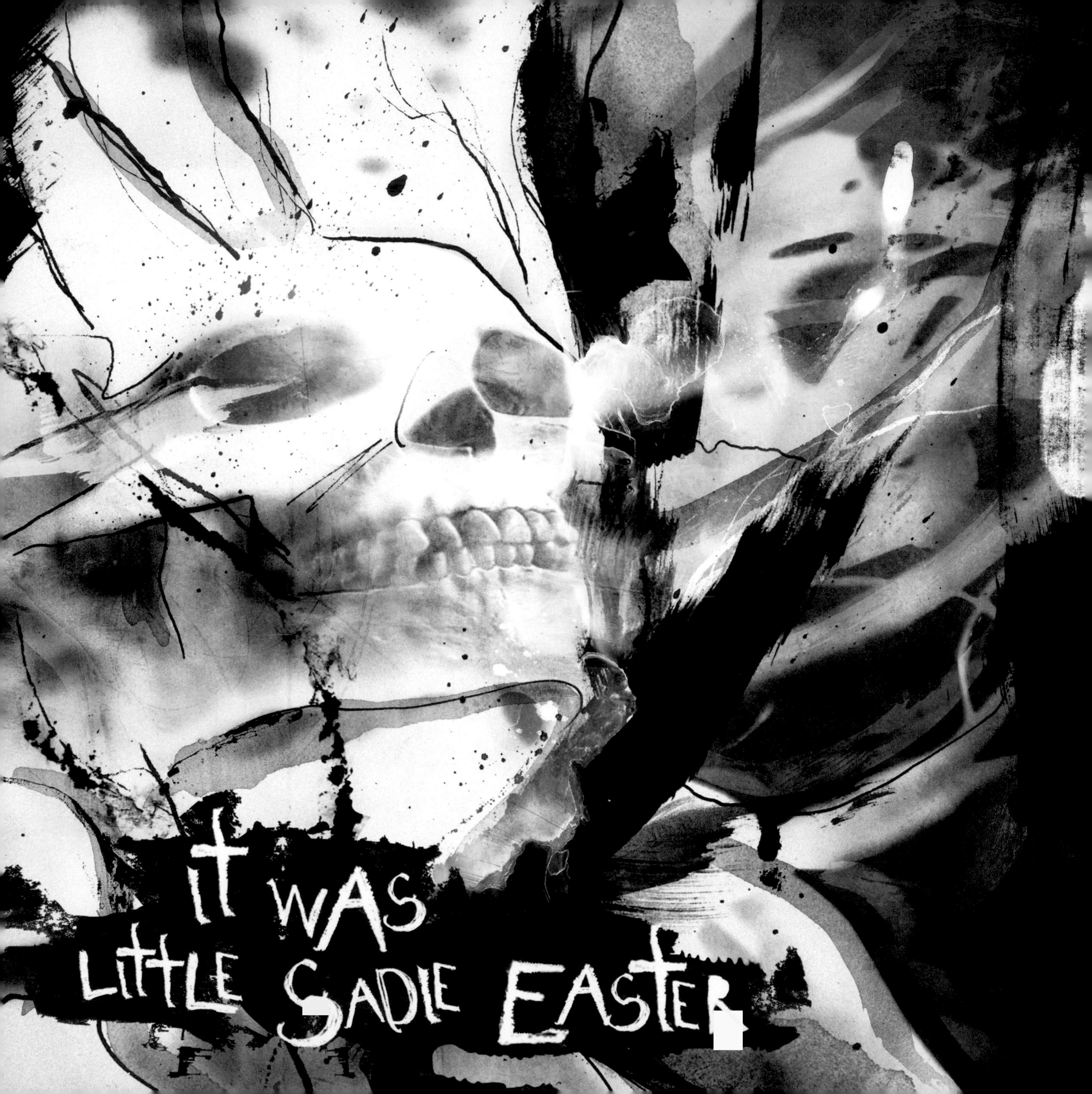
it WAS
LITTLE SADIE EASTER

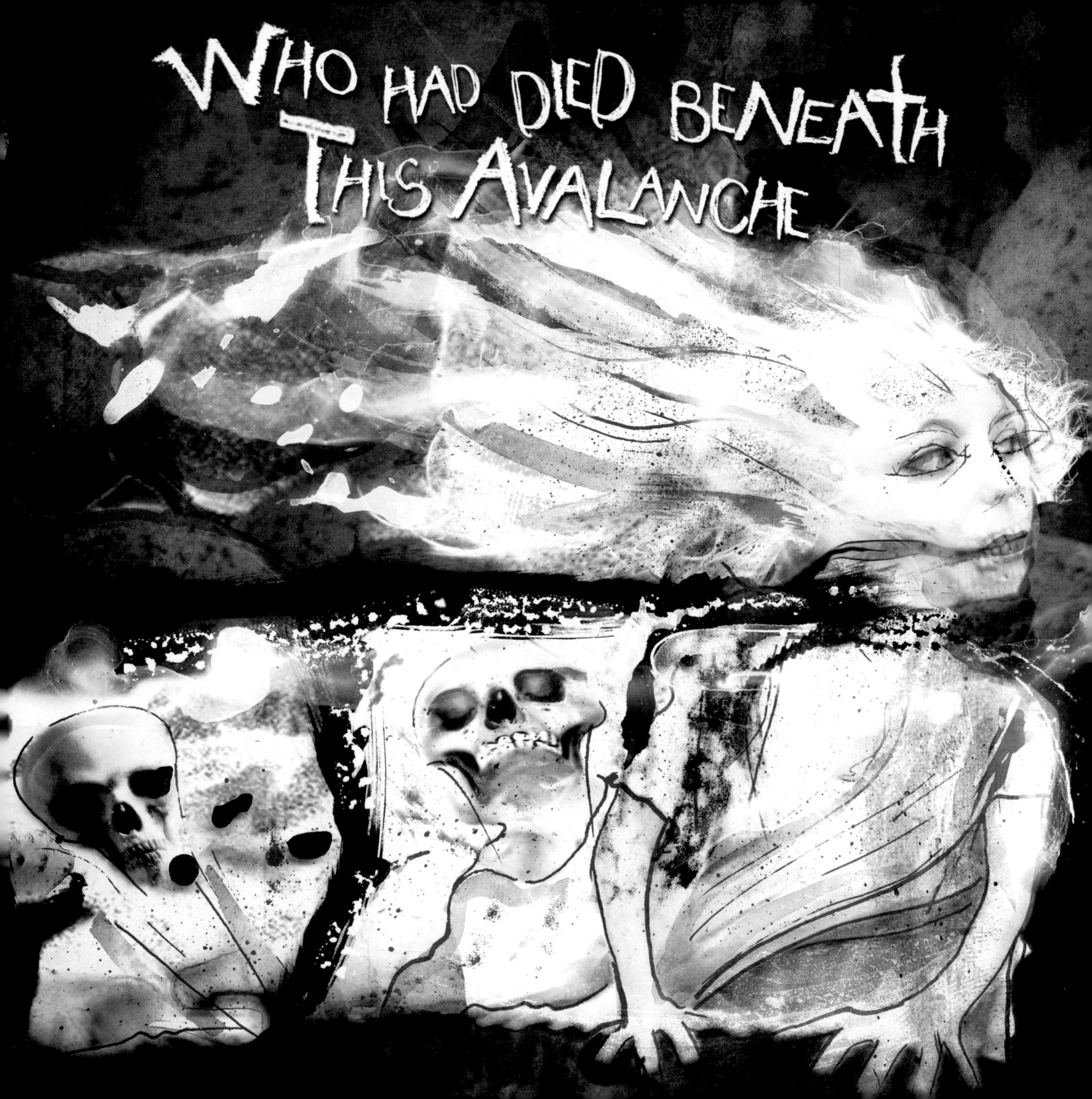
WHO HAD DIED BENEATH
THIS AVALANCHE

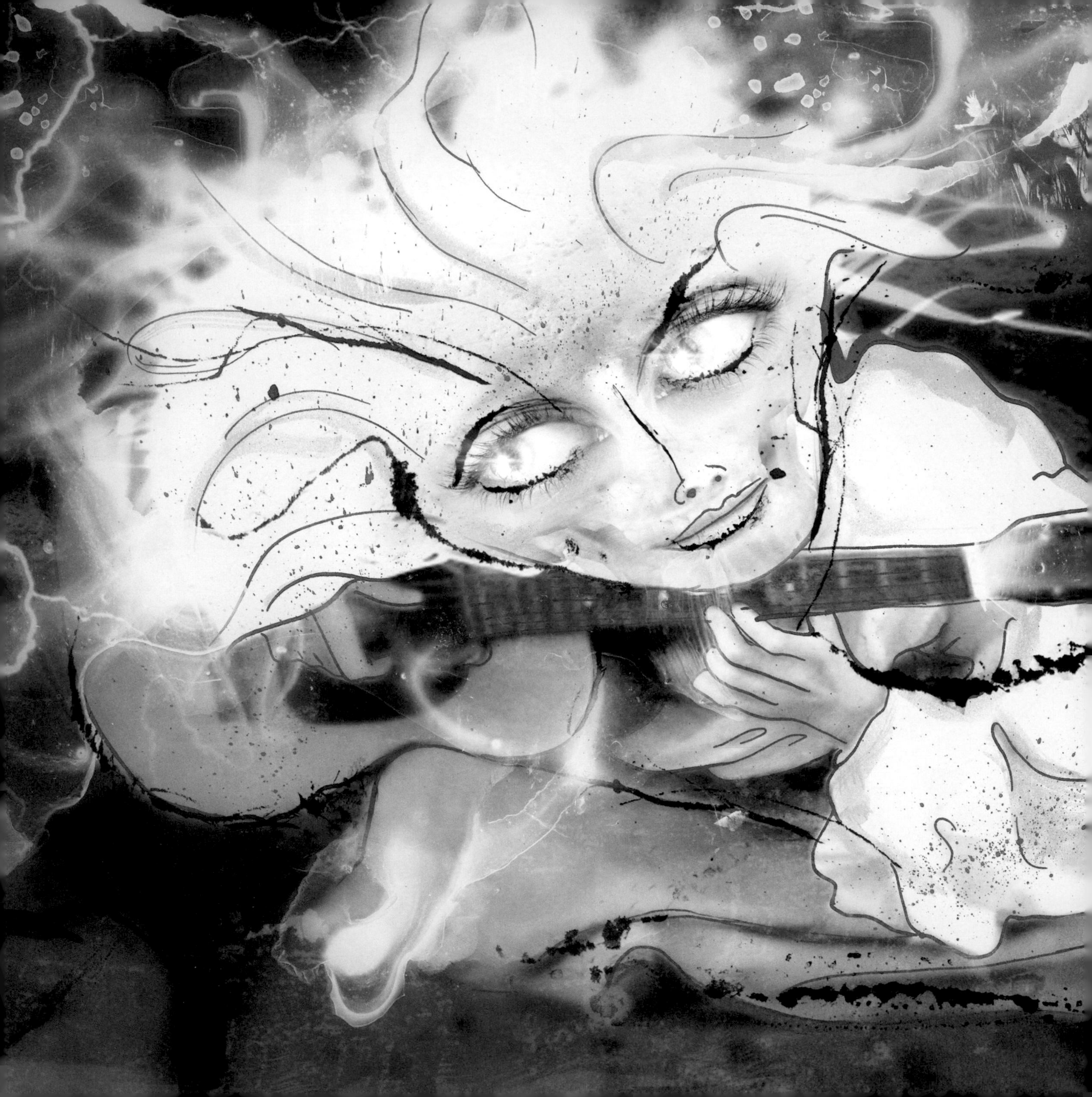

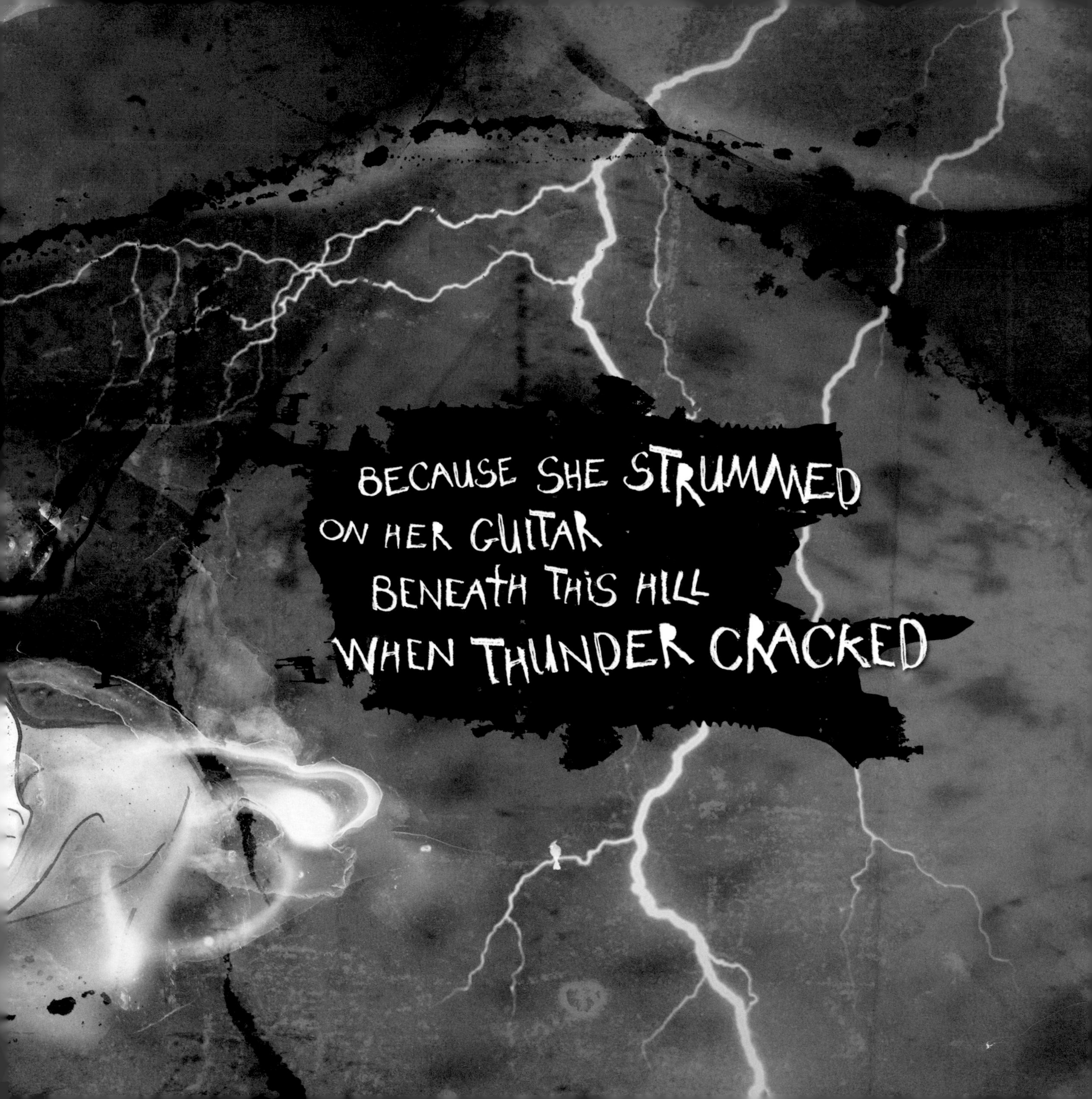

BECAUSE SHE STRUMMED
ON HER GUITAR
BENEATH THIS HILL
WHEN THUNDER CRACKED

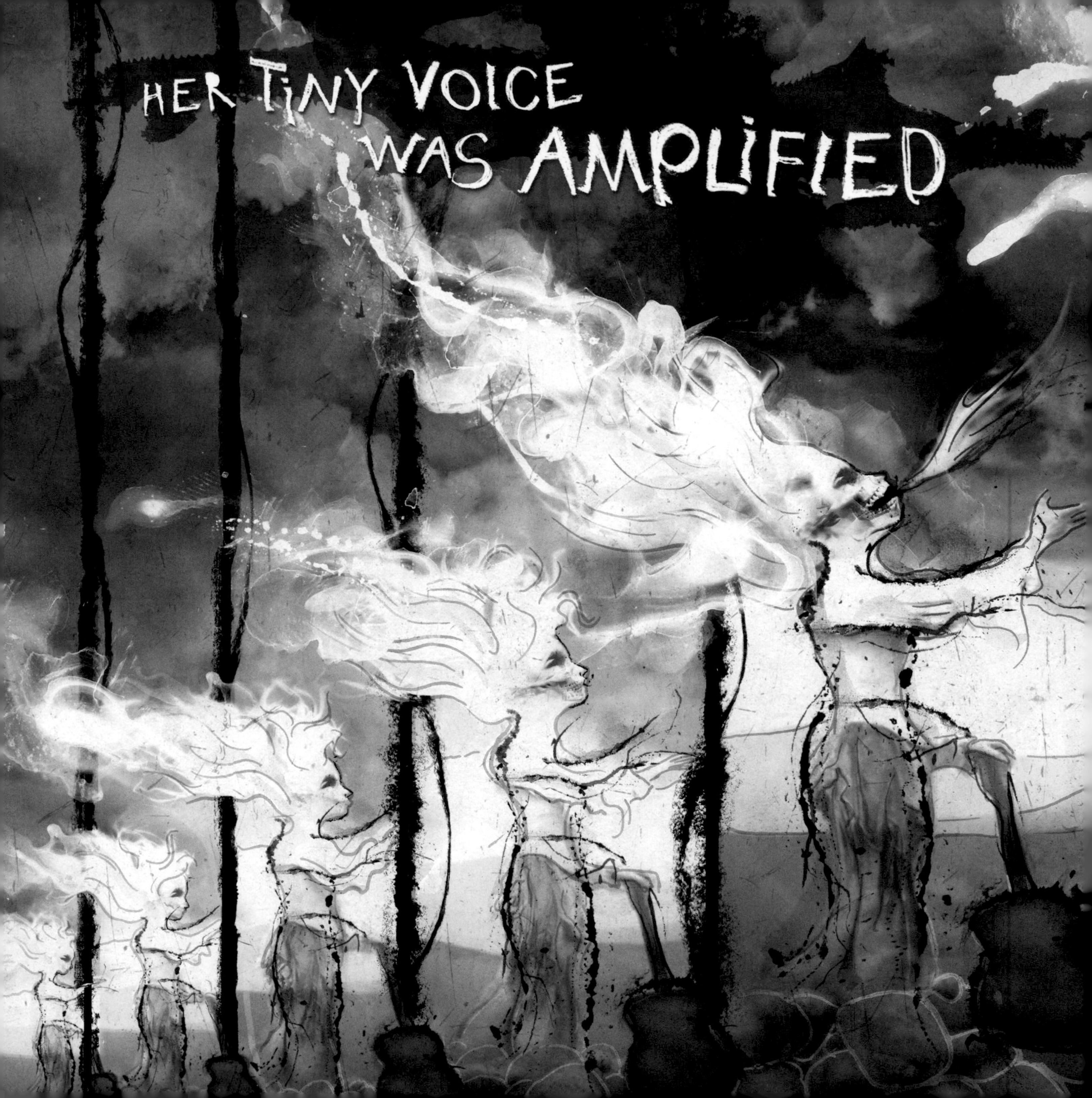
HER TINY VOICE
WAS AMPLIFIED

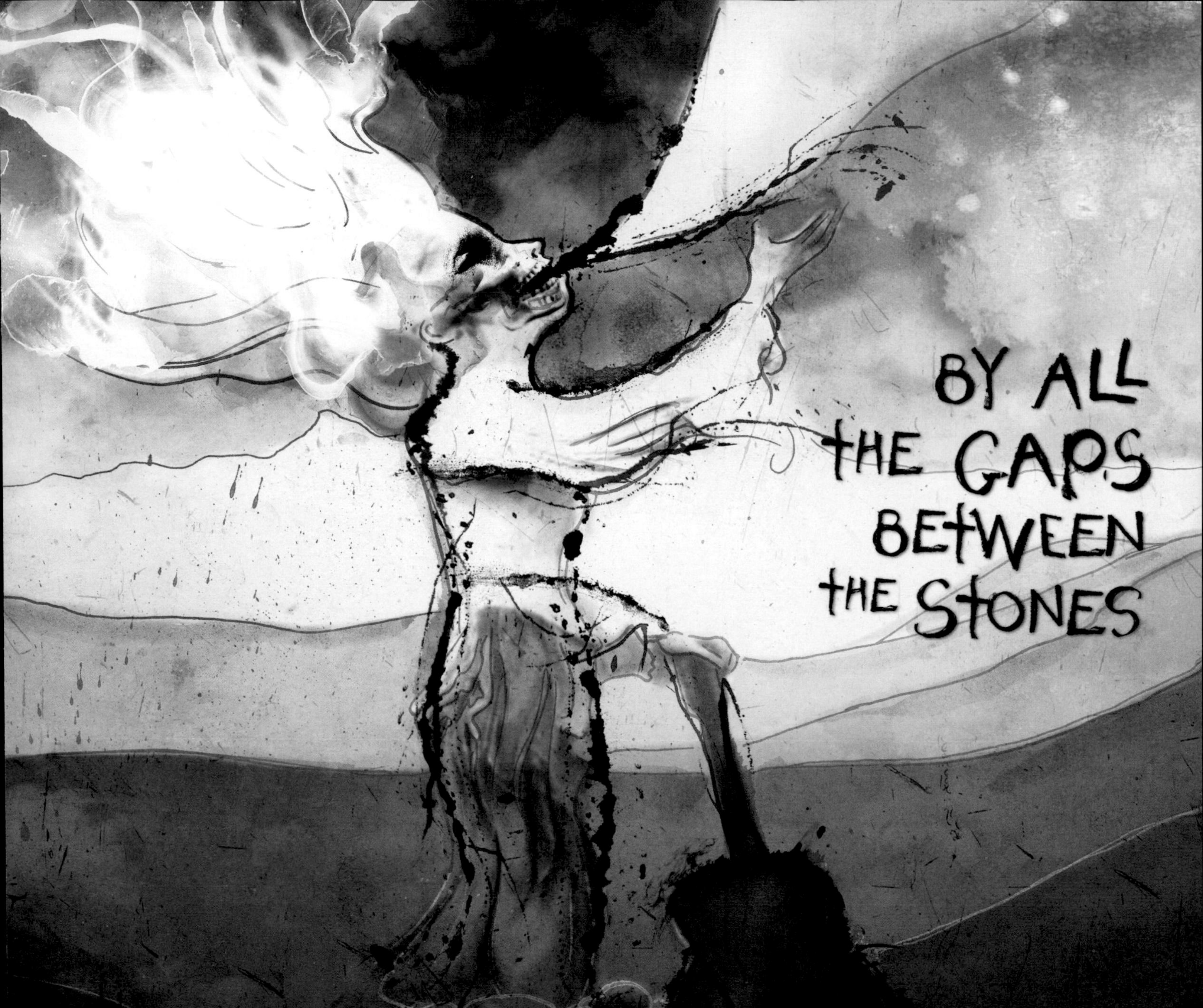
BY ALL
THE GAPS
BETWEEN
THE STONES

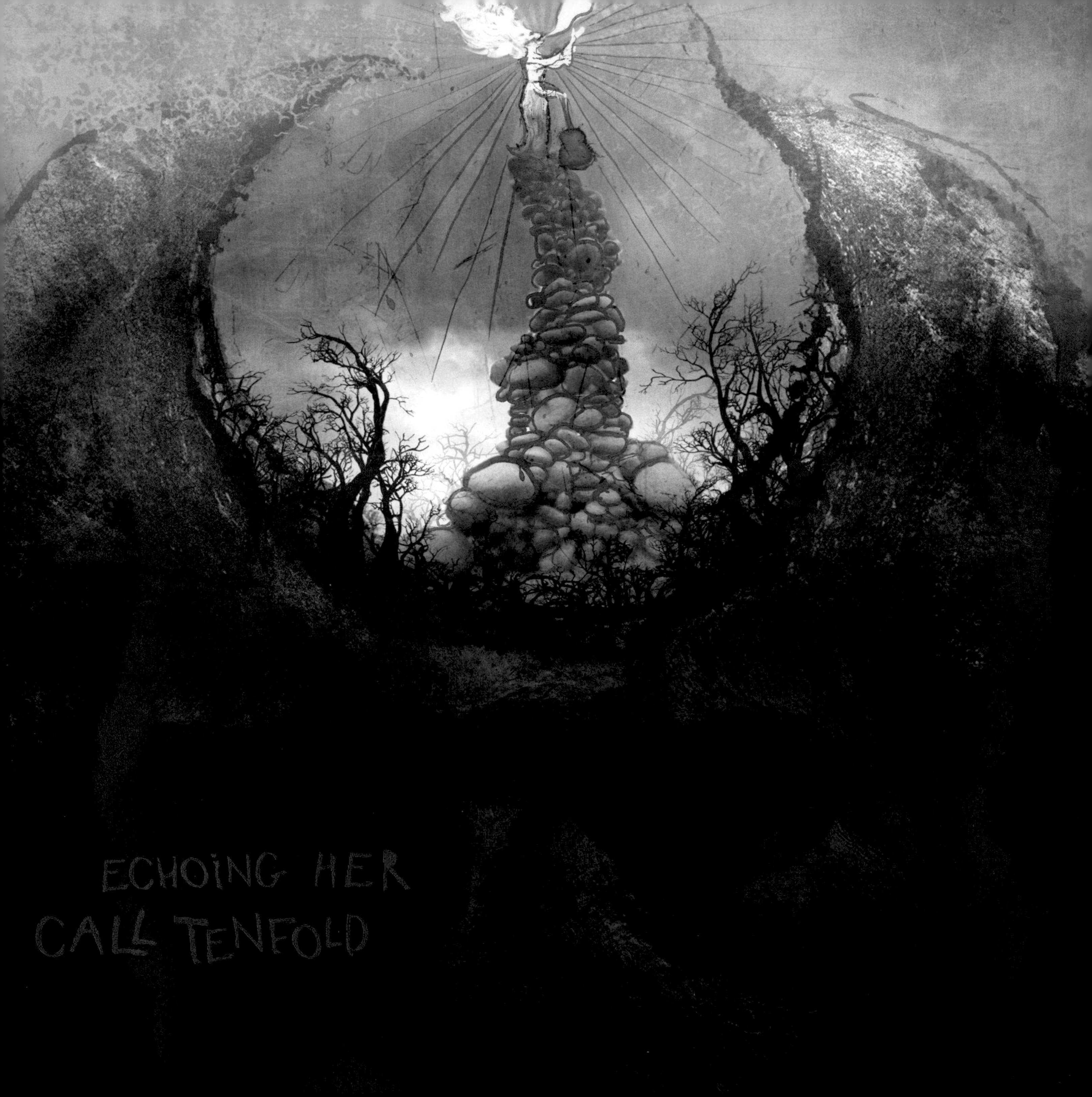

ECHOING HER
CALL TENFOLD

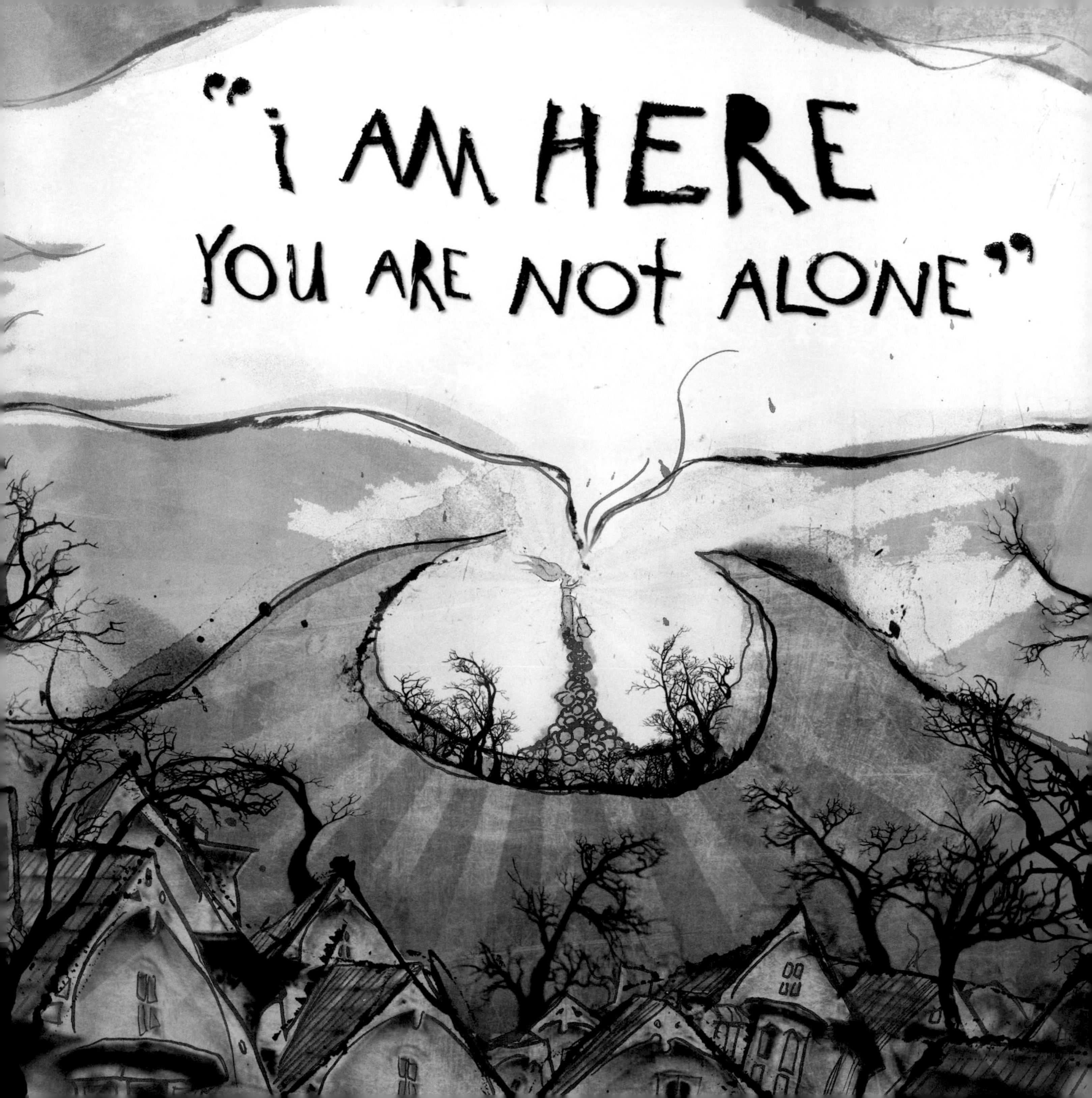
"I AM HERE
YOU ARE NOT ALONE"

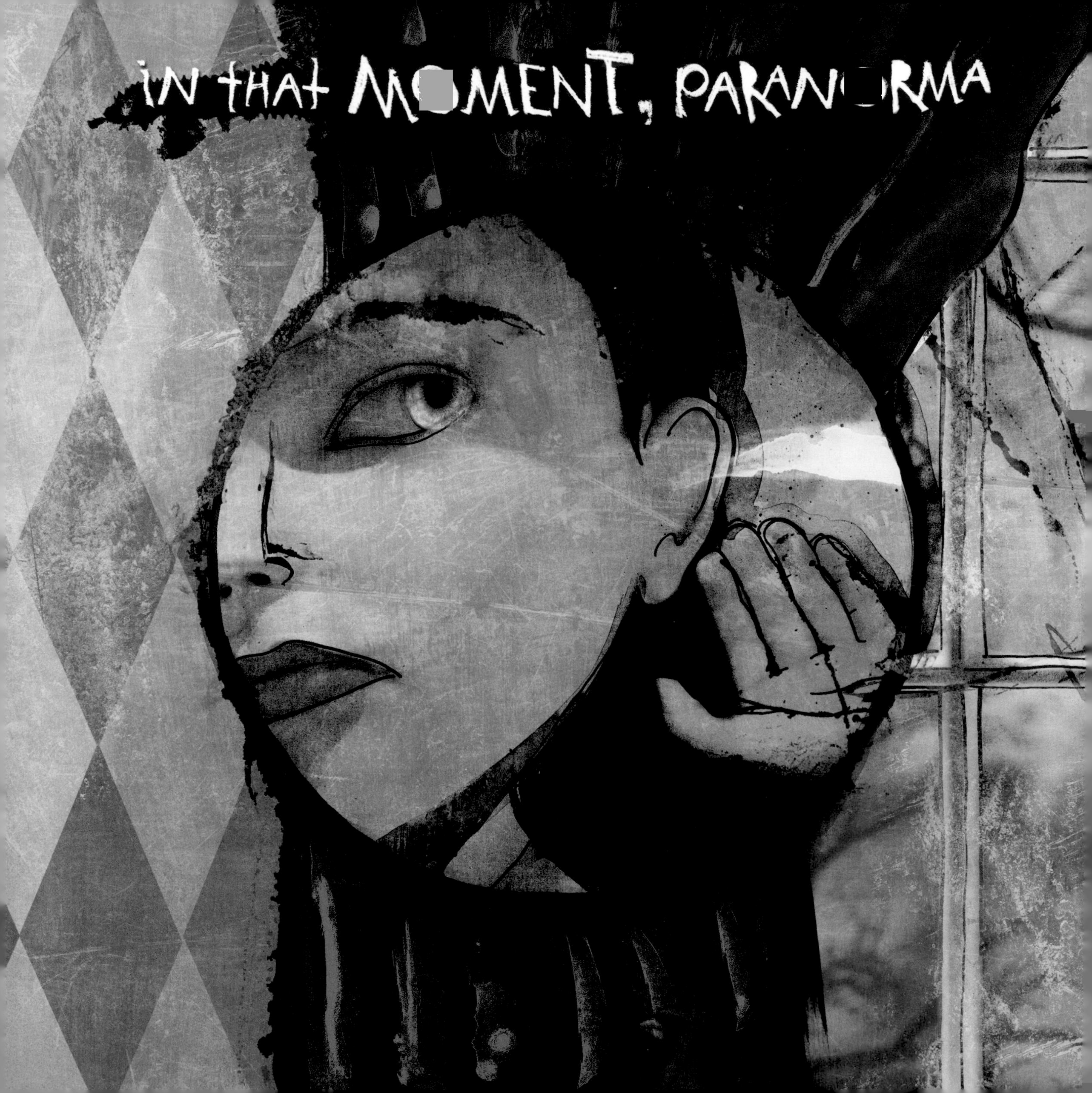
in that MOMENT, PARANORMA

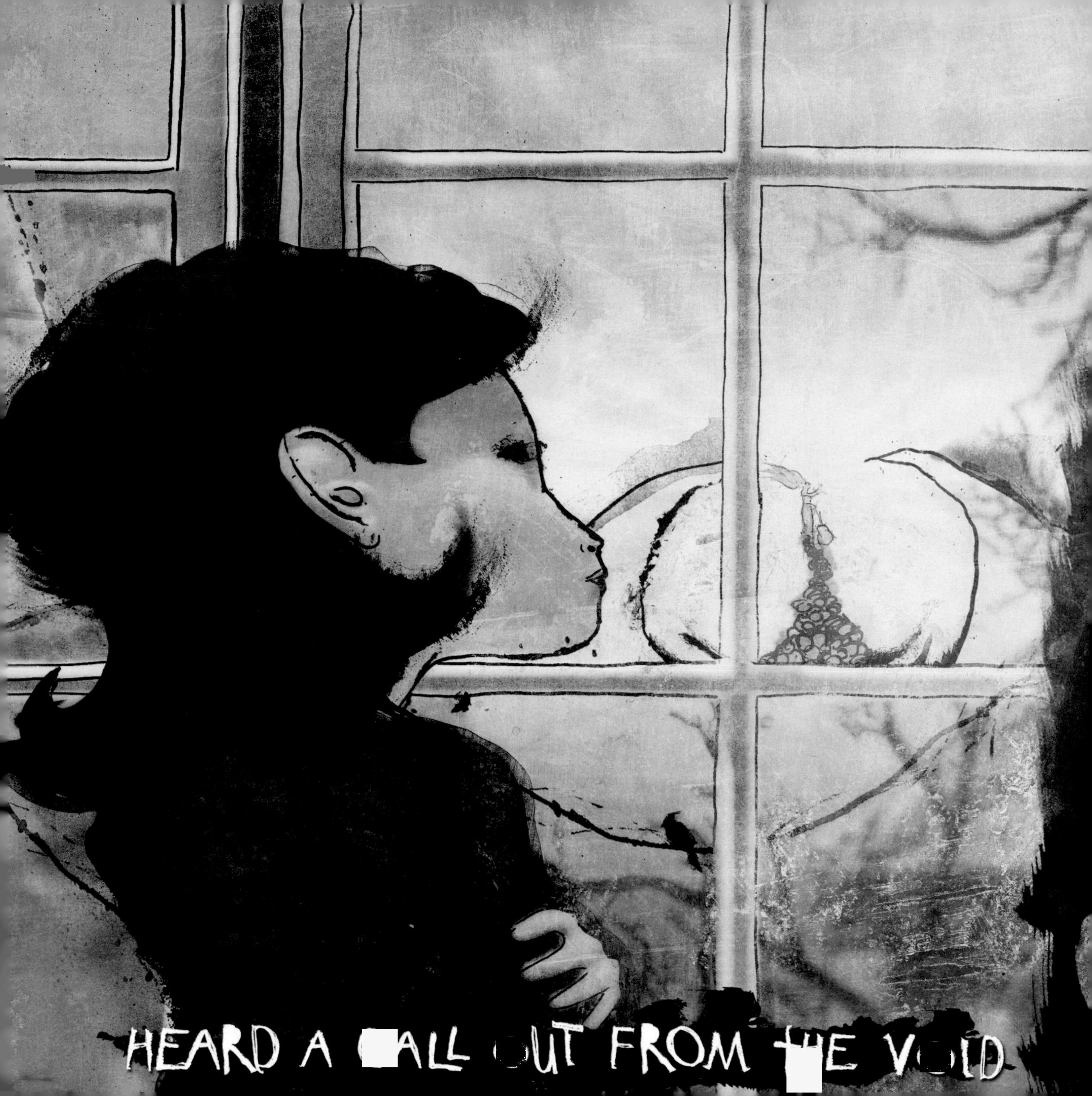
HEARD A CALL OUT FROM THE V[redacted]ID

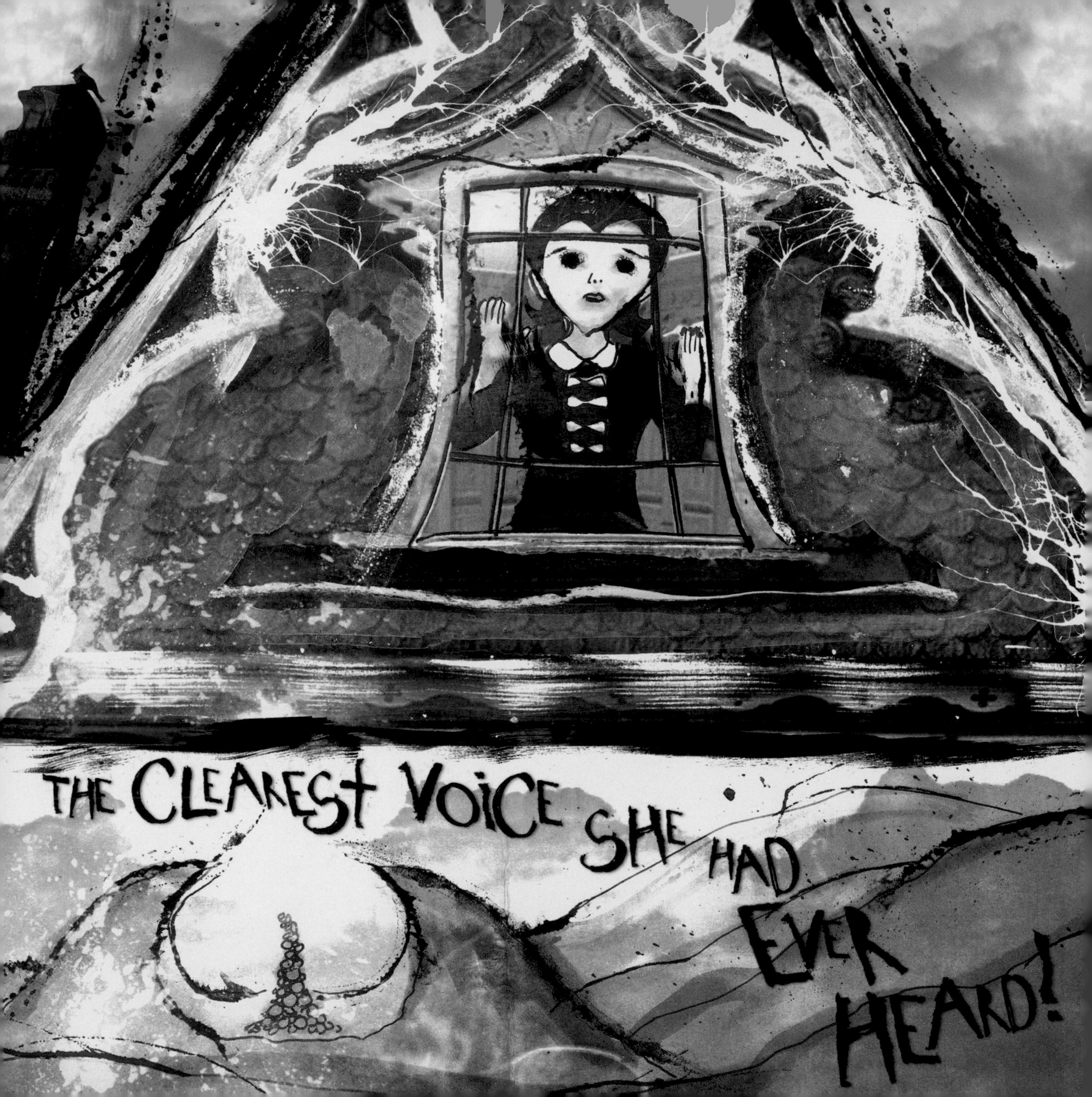
THE CLEAREST VOICE SHE HAD EVER HEARD!

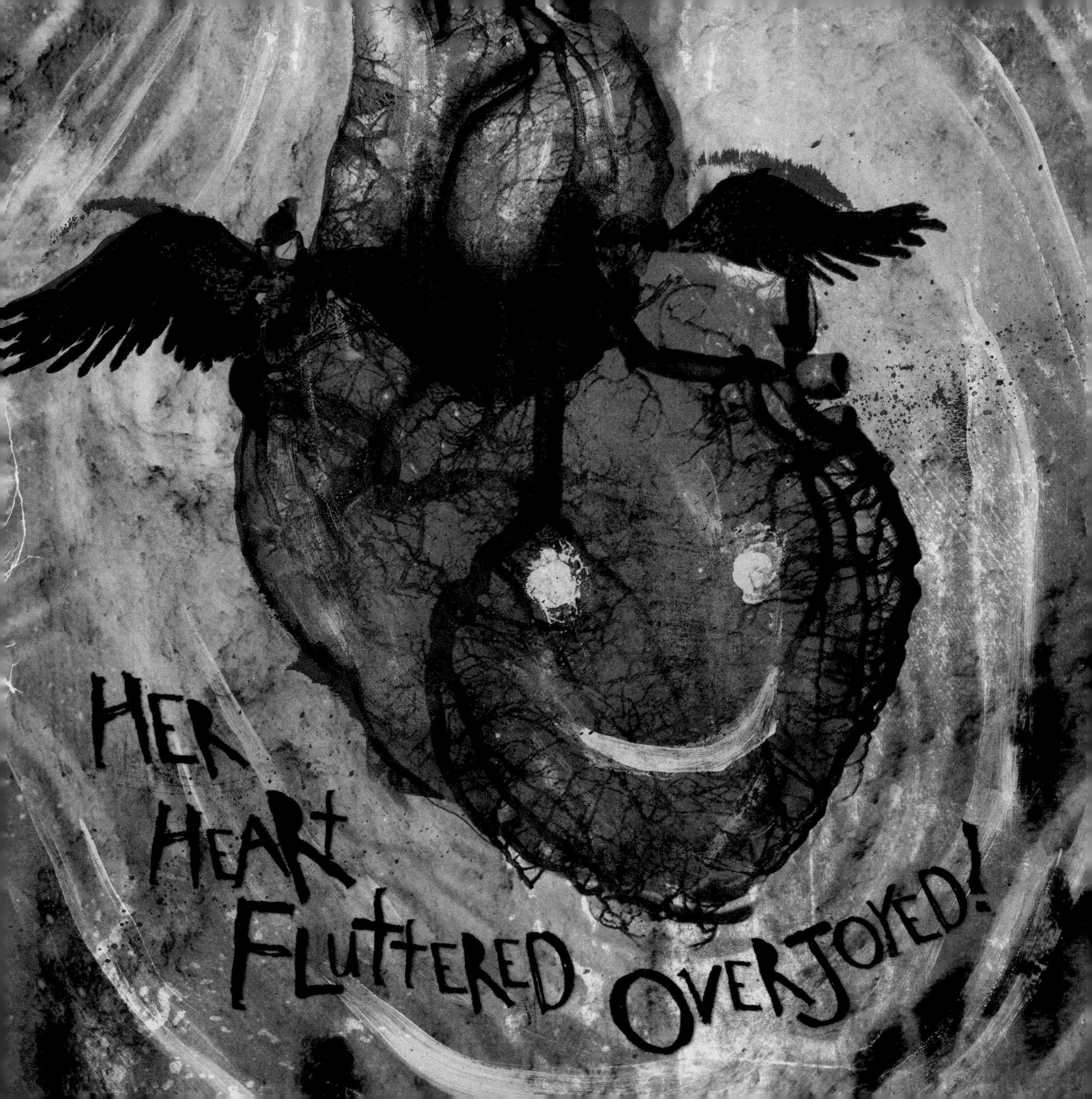
HER
HEART
FLUTTERED
OVERJOYED!

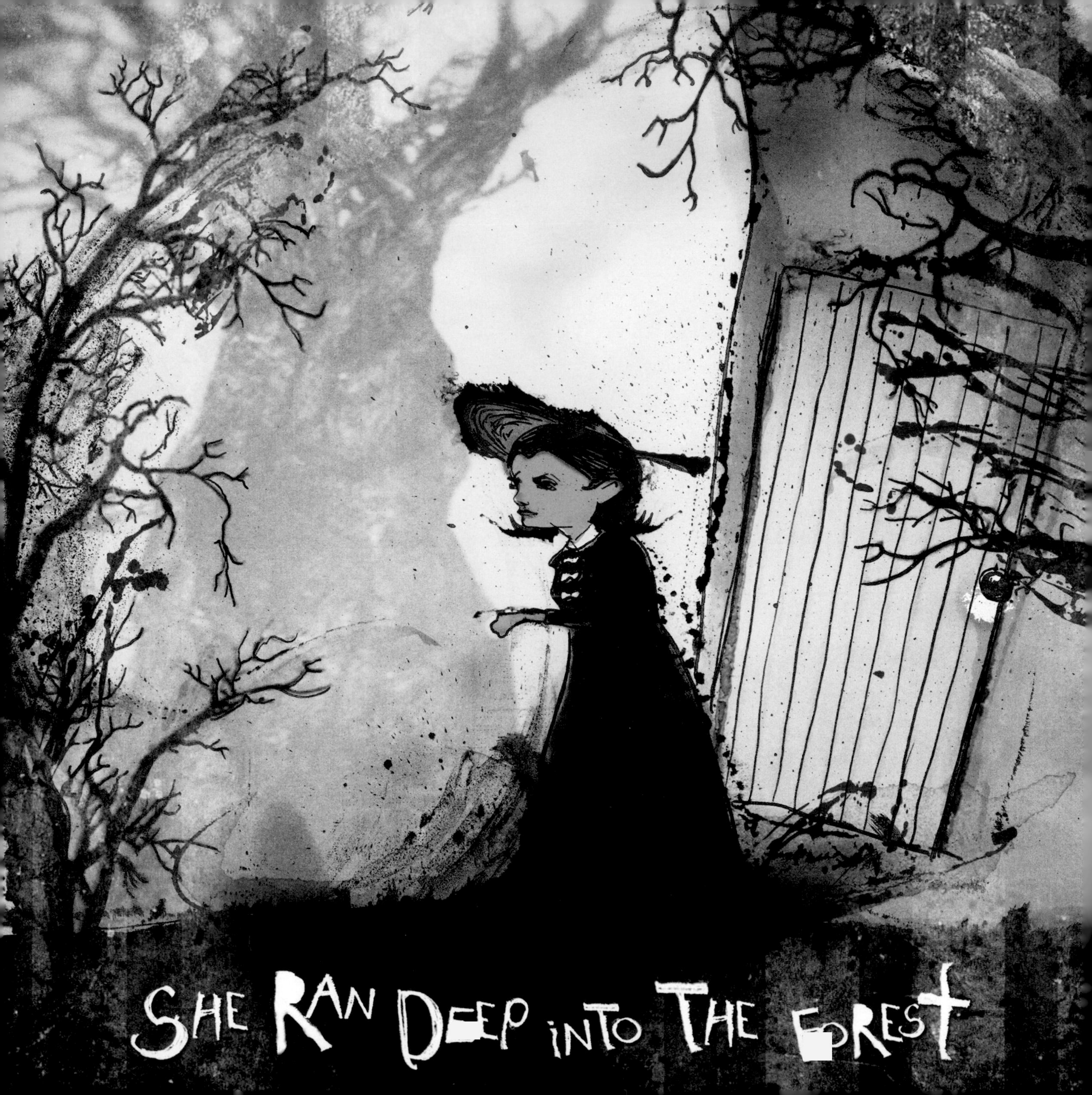
SHE RAN DEEP INTO THE FOREST

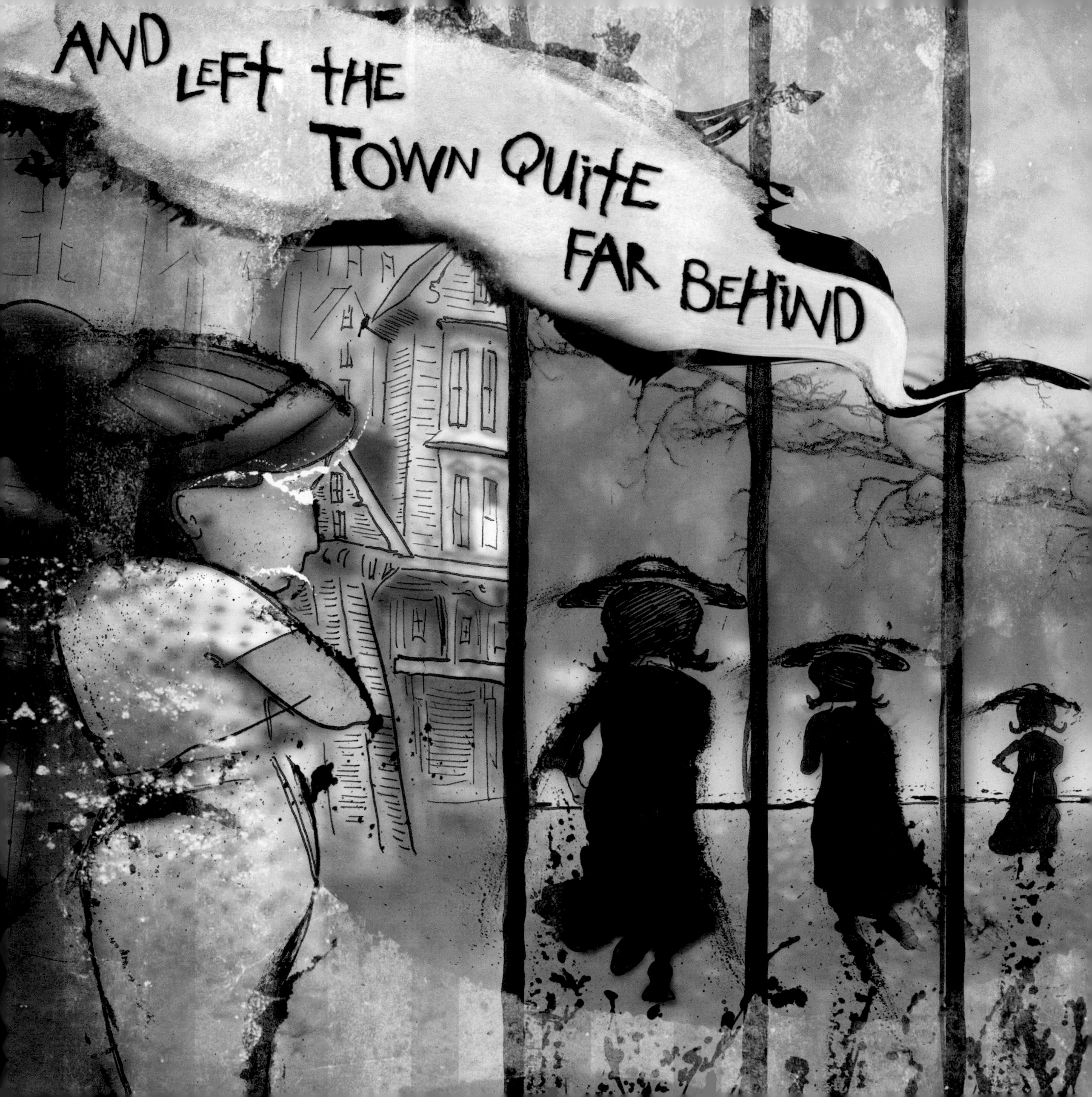
AND LEFT THE TOWN QUITE FAR BEHIND

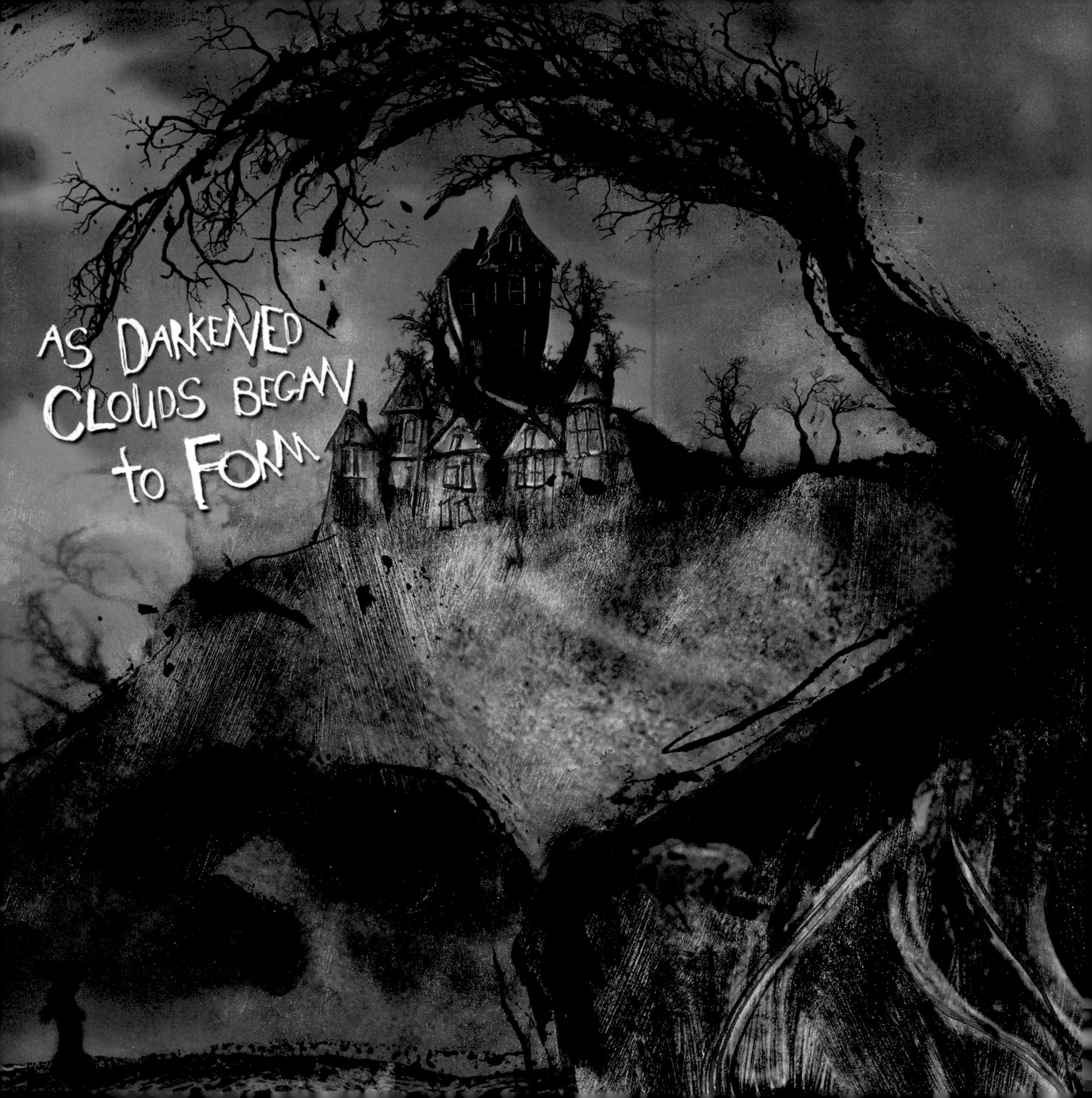
AS DARKENED
CLOUDS BEGAN
to FORM

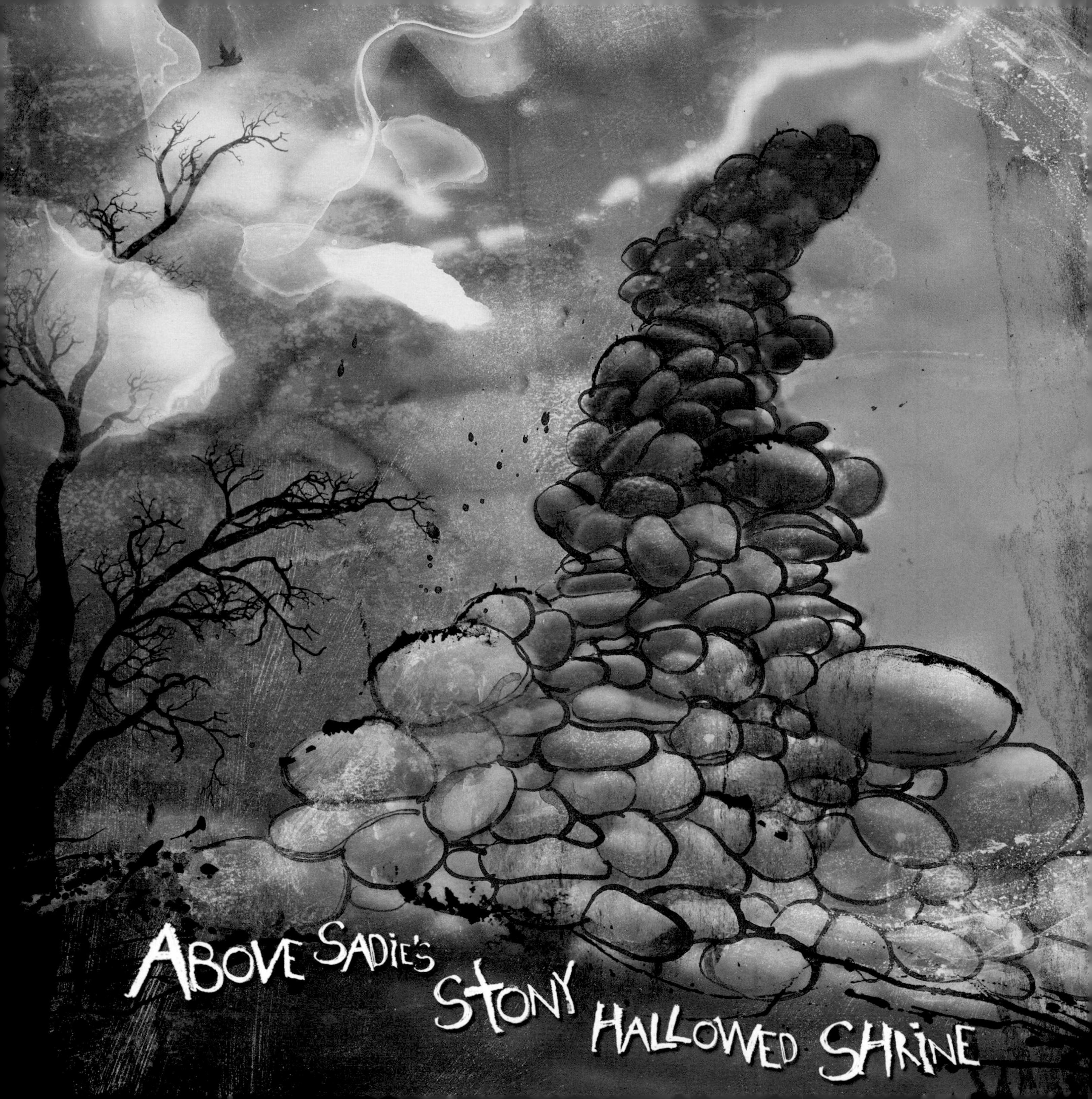
ABOVE SADIE'S STONY HALLOWED SHRINE

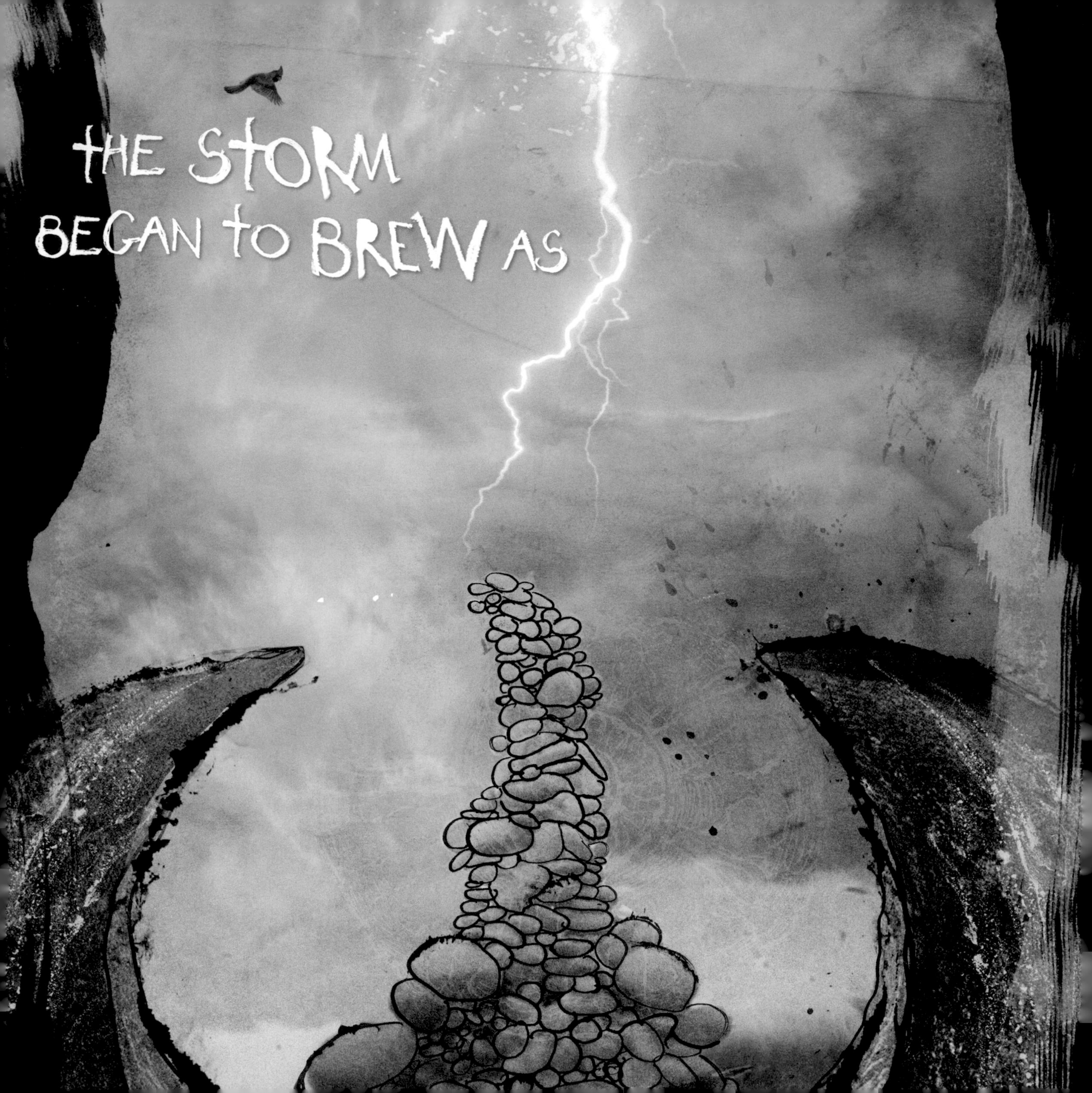

the storm began to brew as

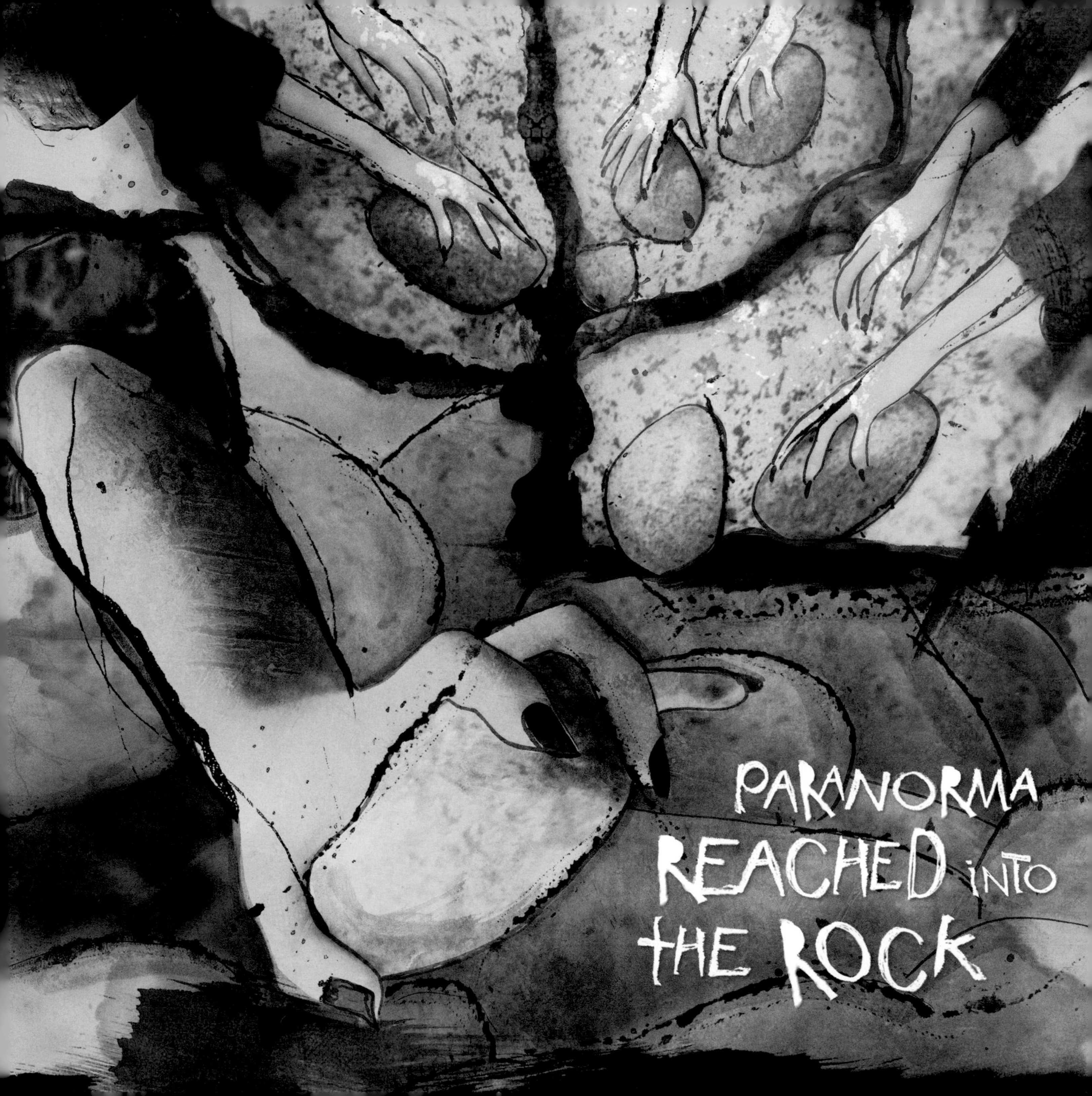
PARANORMA
REACHED INTO
THE ROCK

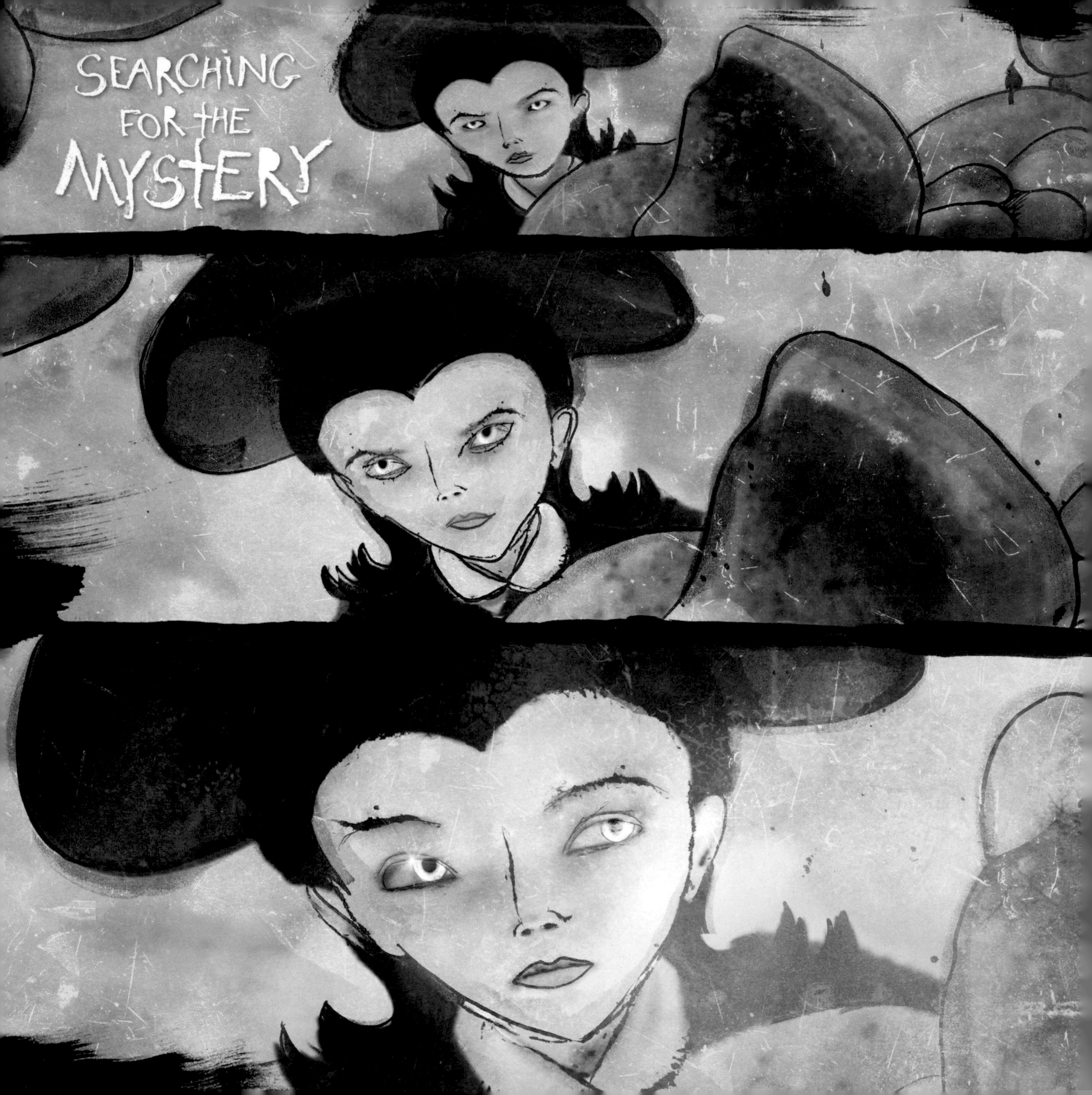
SEARCHING FOR THE MYSTERY

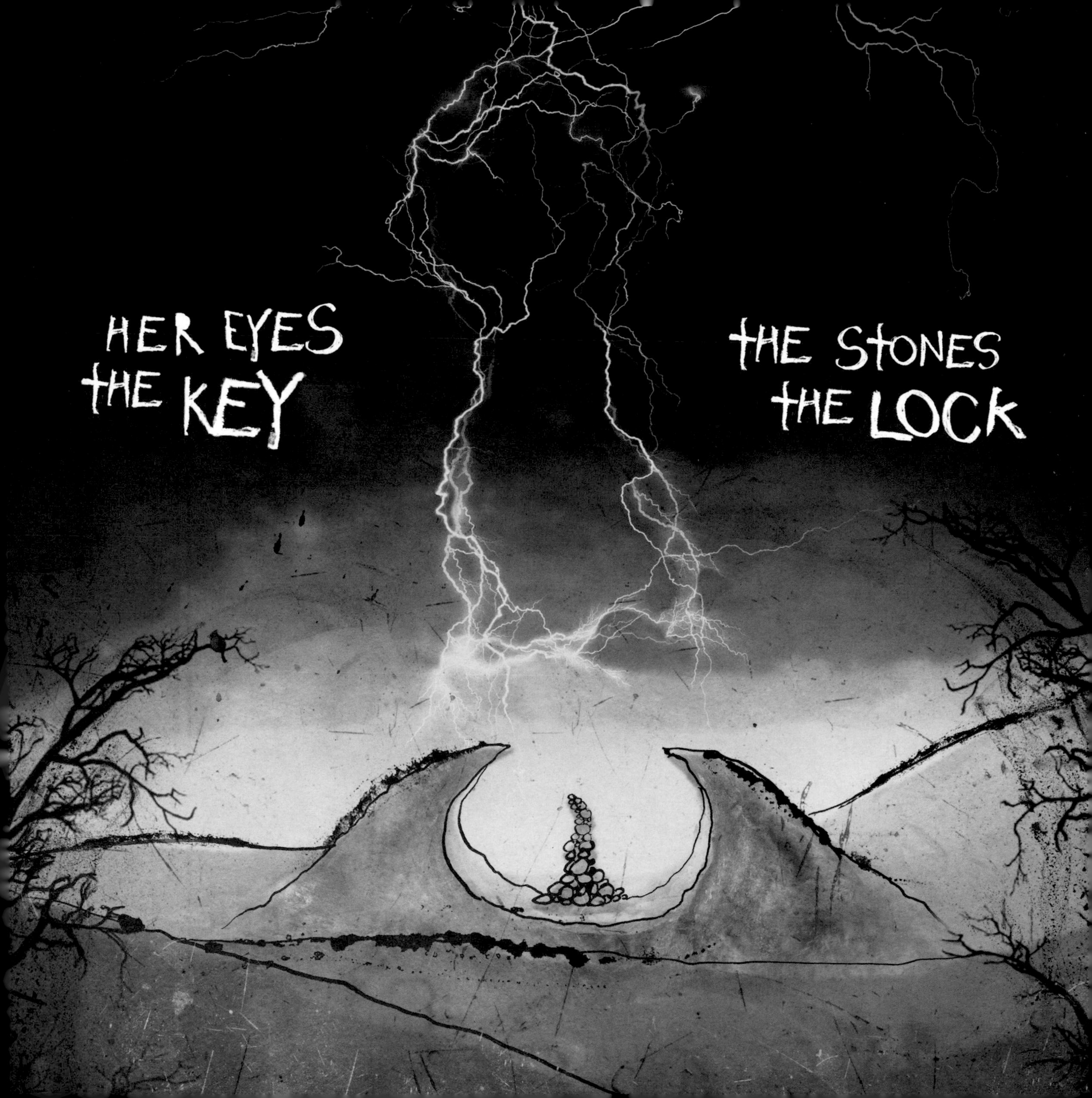
HER EYES
THE KEY
THE STONES
THE LOCK

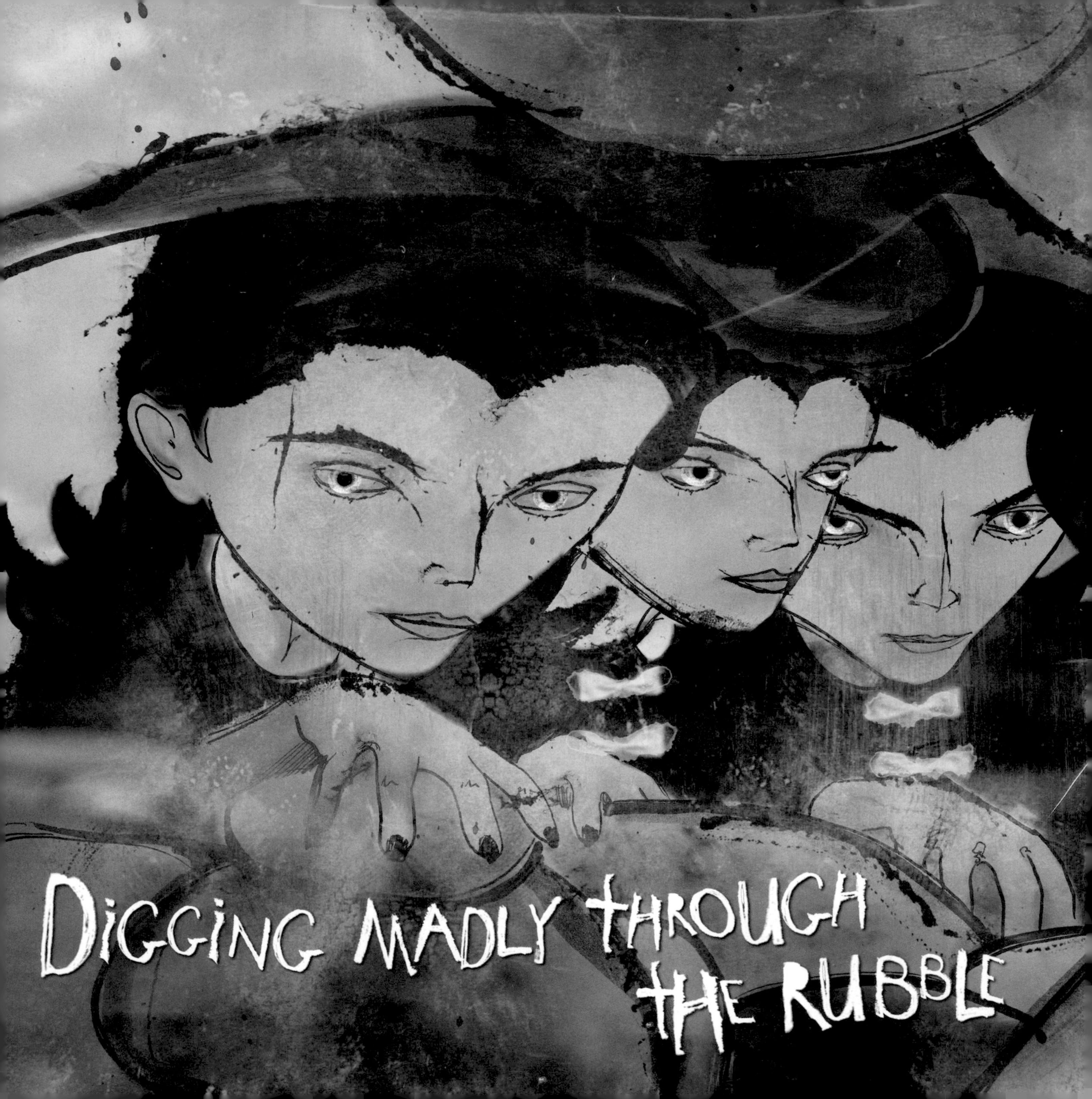
DIGGING MADLY THROUGH THE RUBBLE

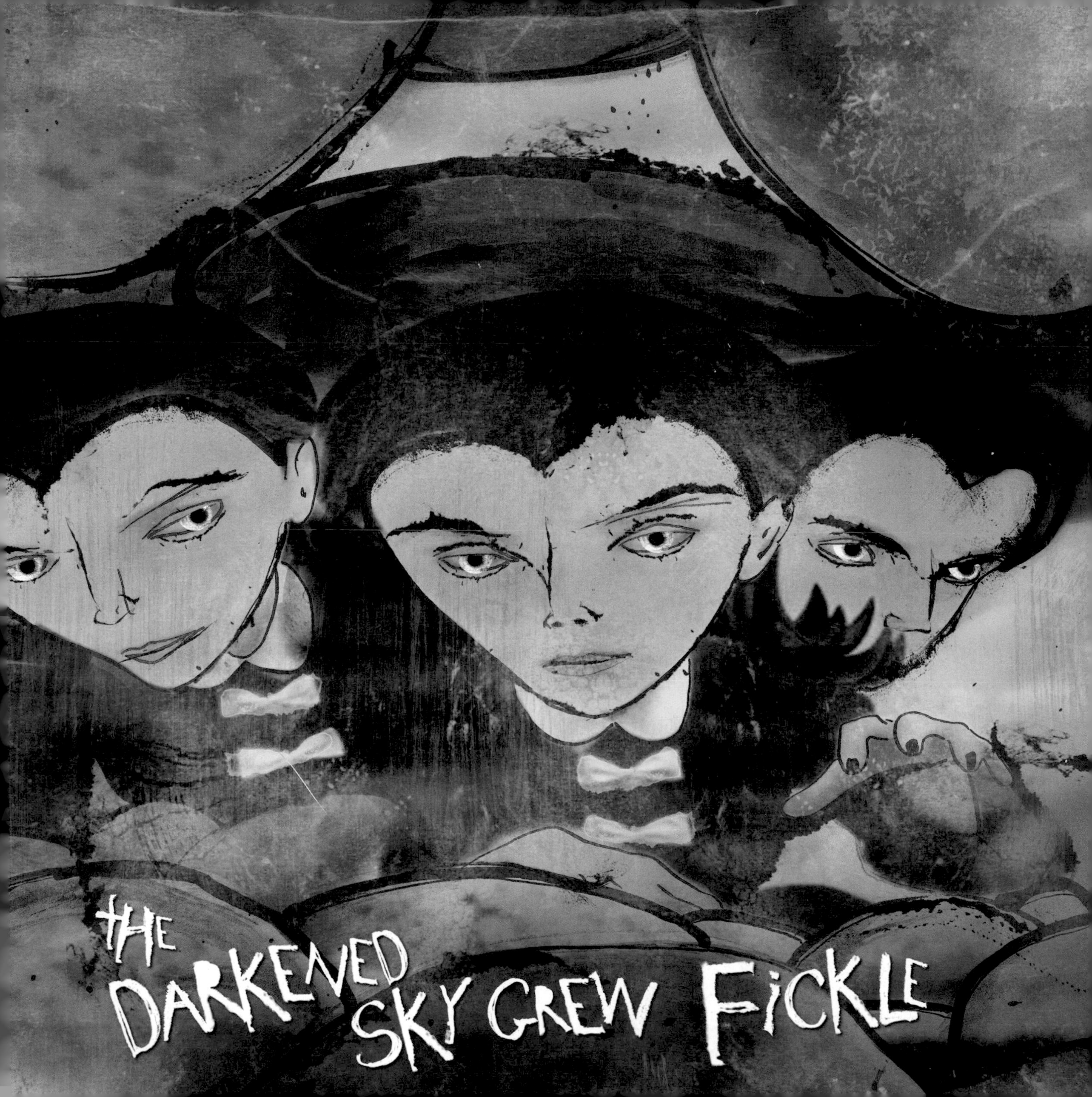
THE DARKENED SKY GREW FICKLE

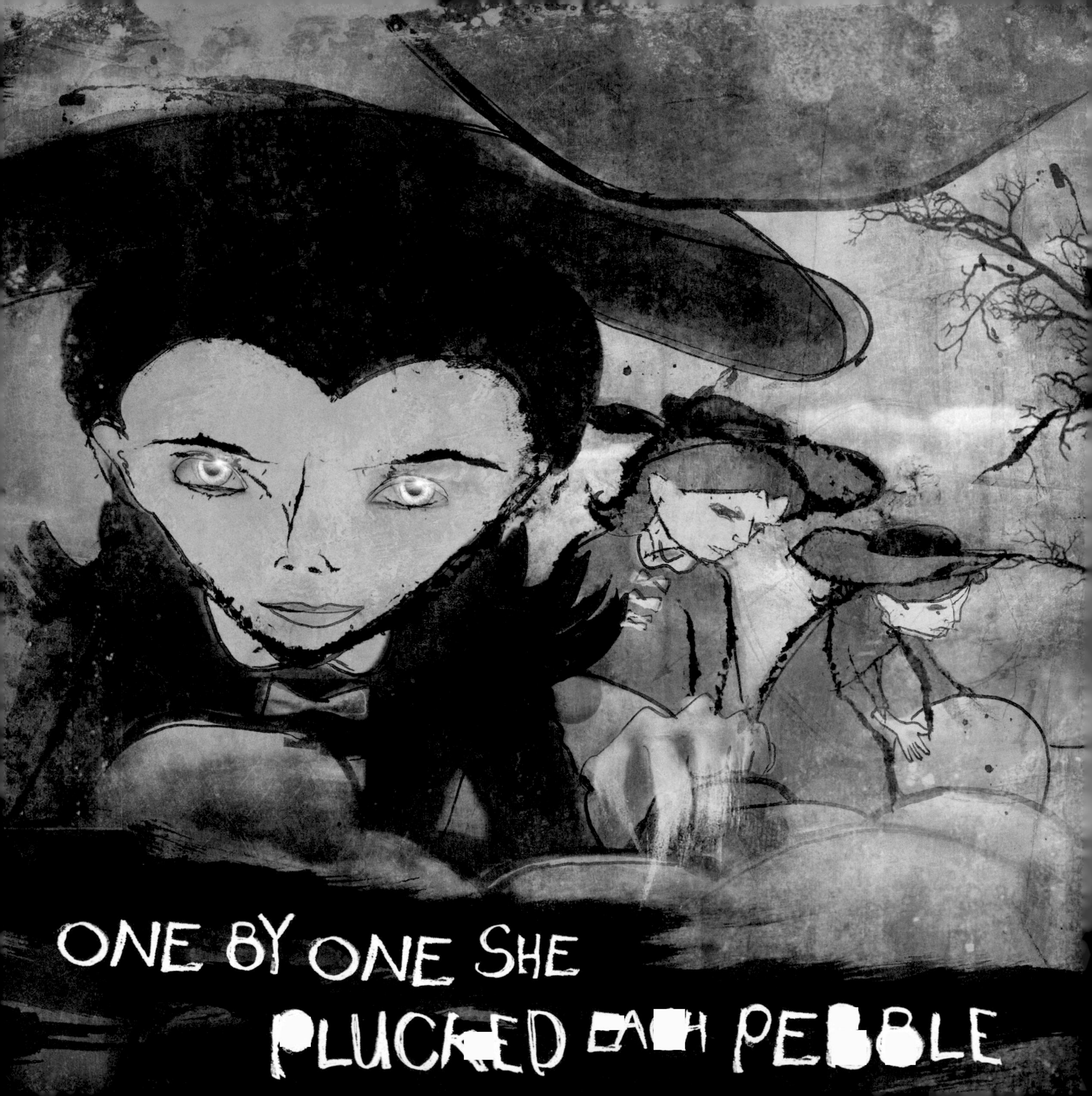
ONE BY ONE SHE
PLUCKED EACH PEBBLE

AS MISS SADIE FASTER OGLED

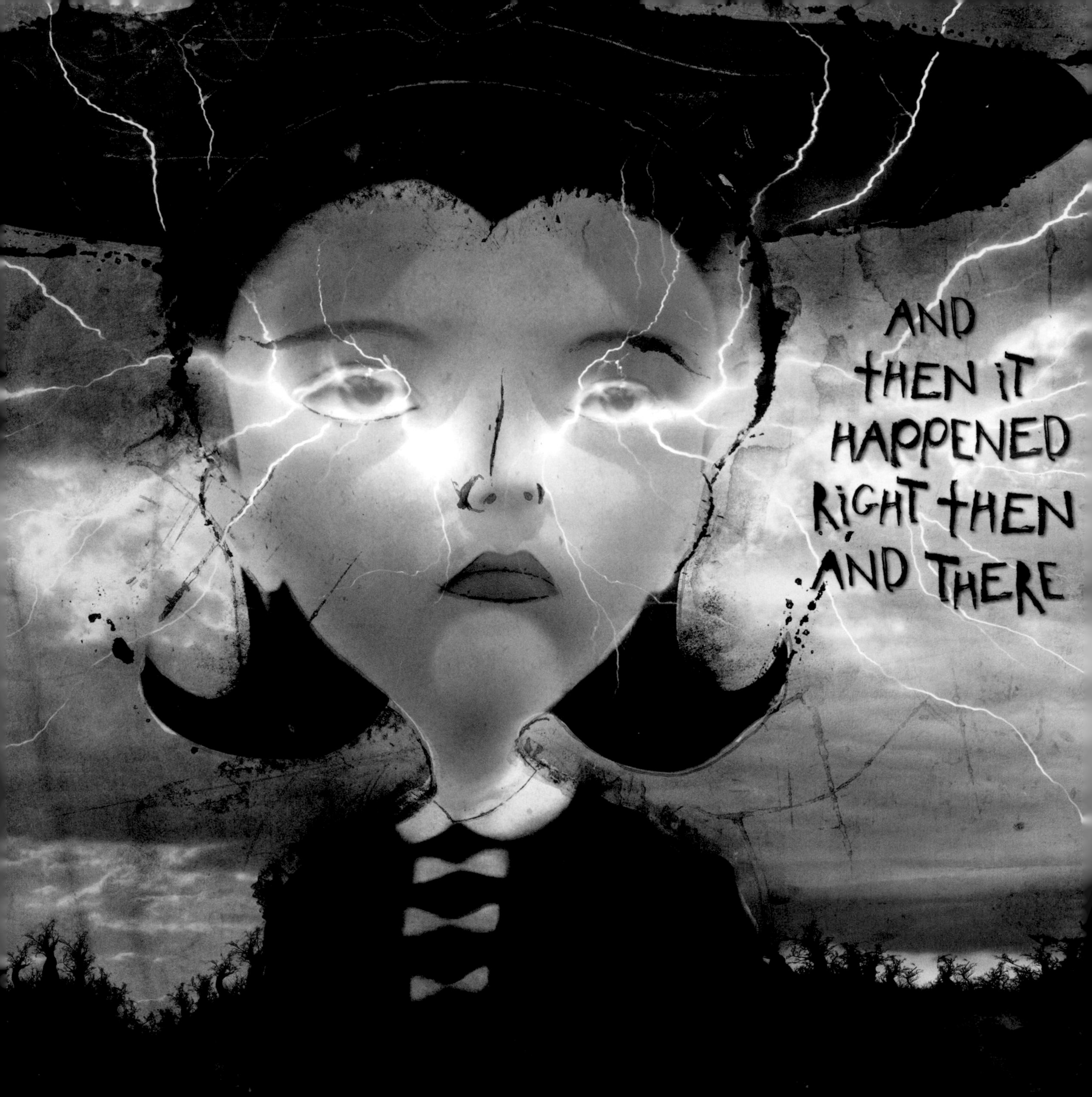

AND THEN IT HAPPENED RIGHT THEN AND THERE

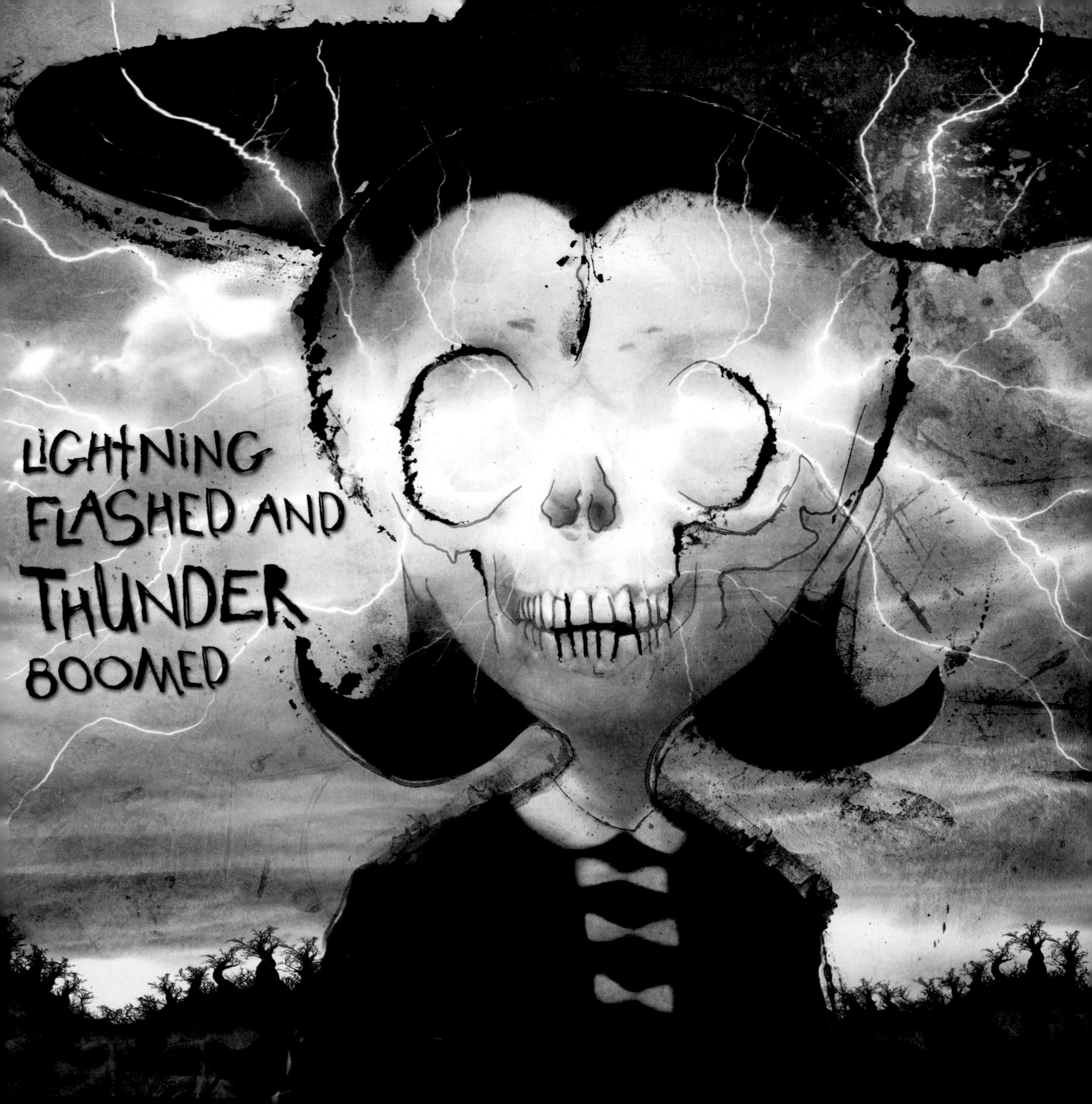
LIGHTNING FLASHED AND THUNDER BOOMED

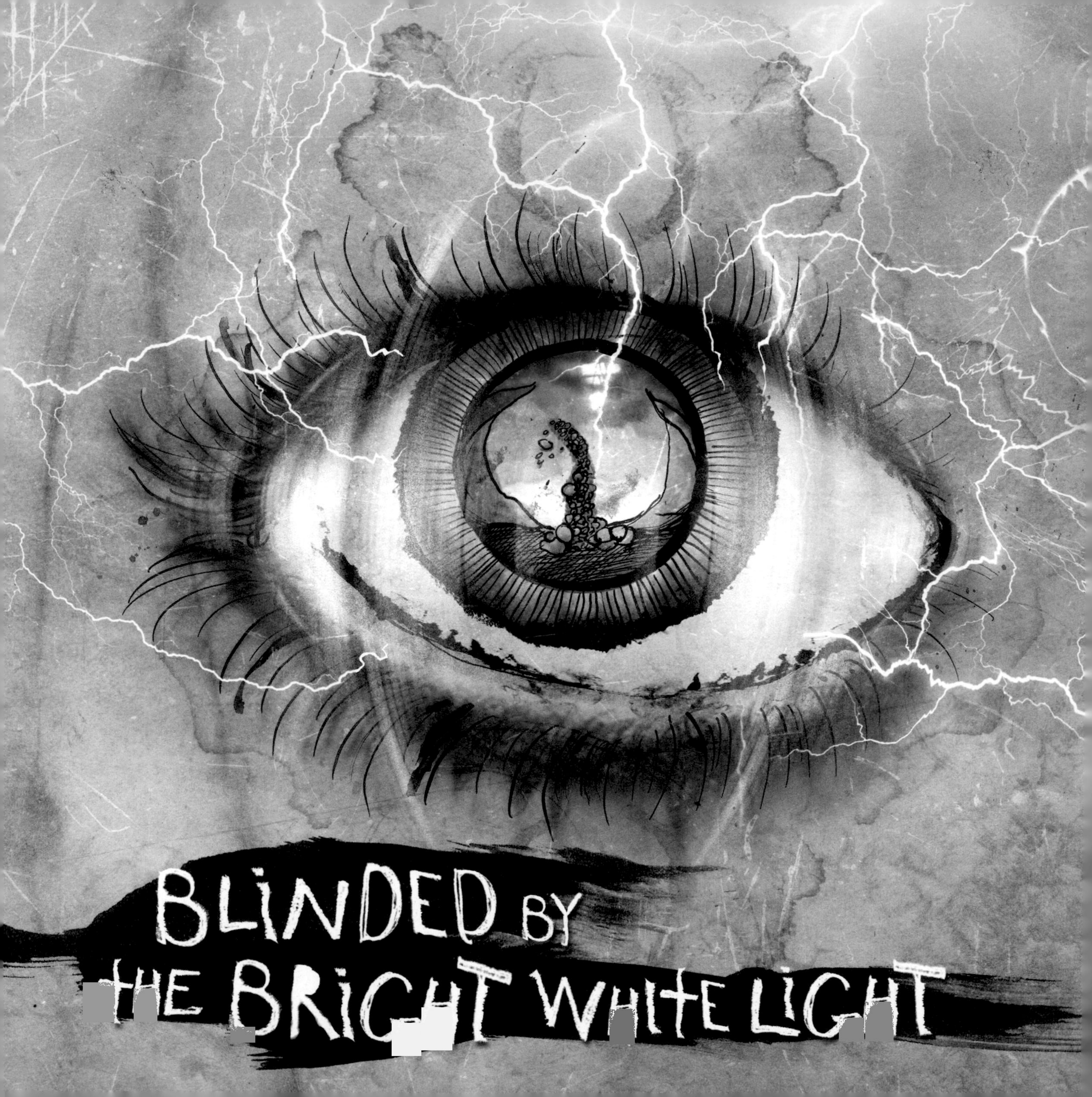
BLINDED BY
THE BRIGHT WHITE LIGHT

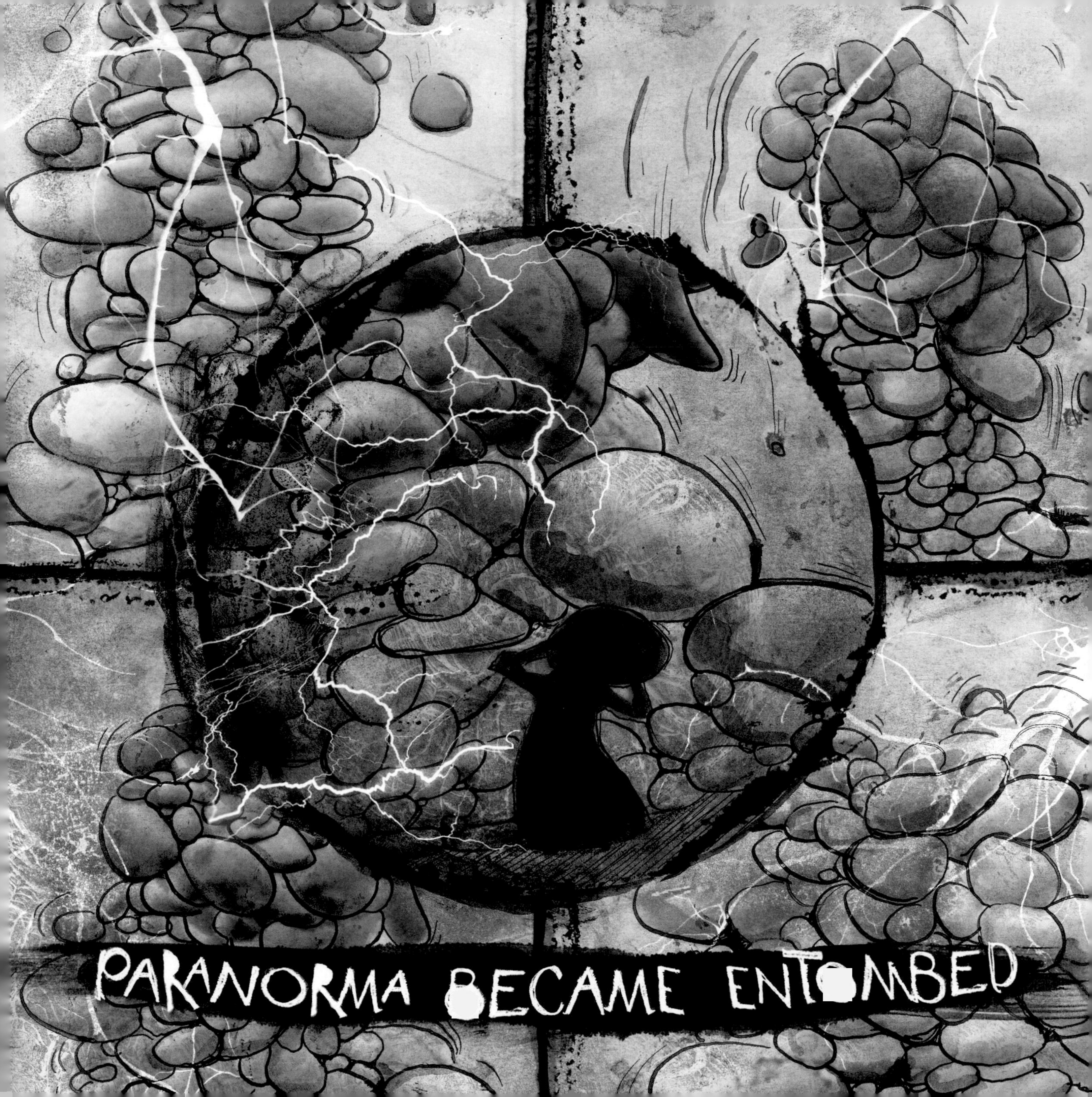
PARANORMA BECAME ENTOMBED

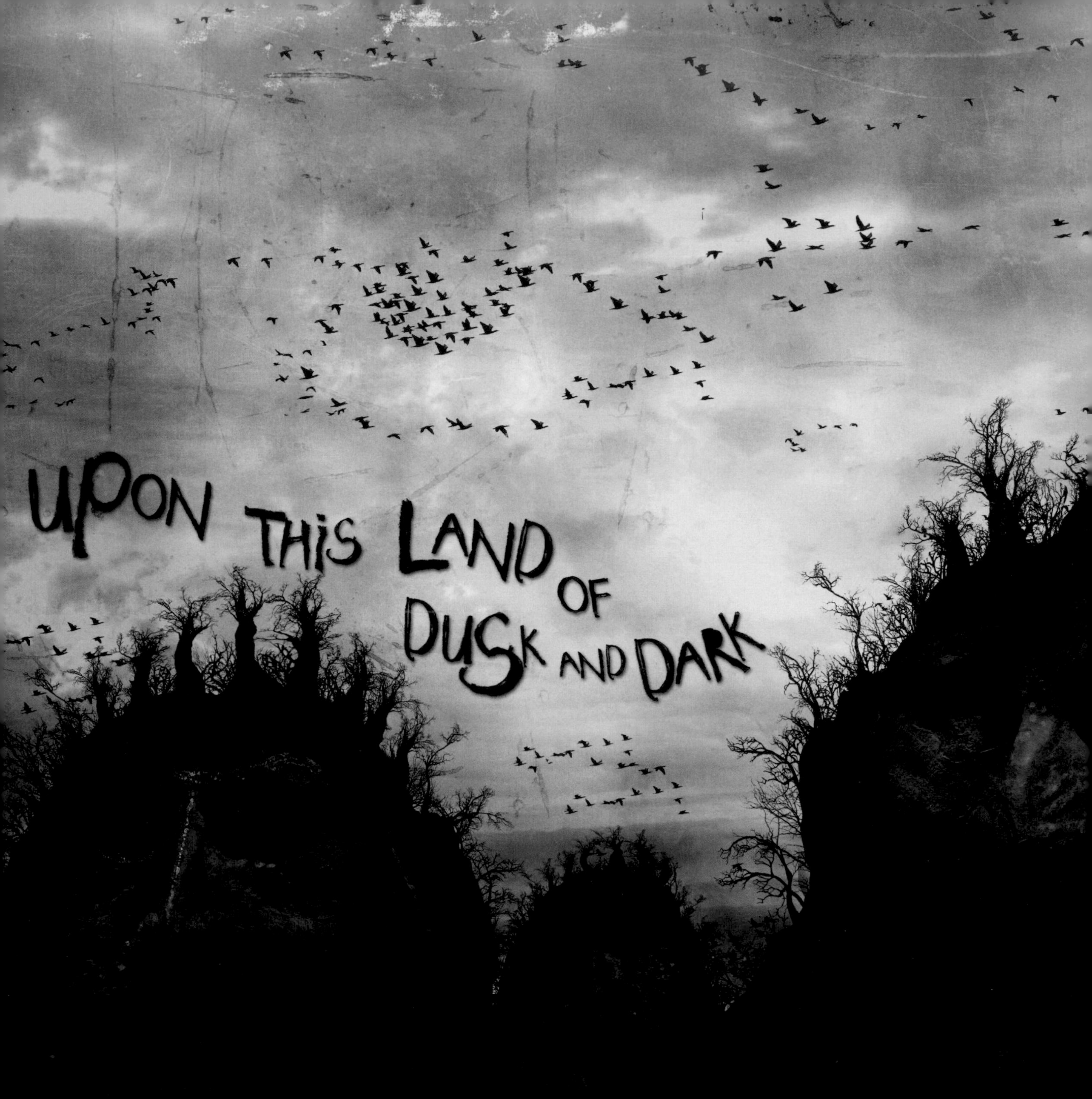
UPON THIS LAND OF DUSK AND DARK

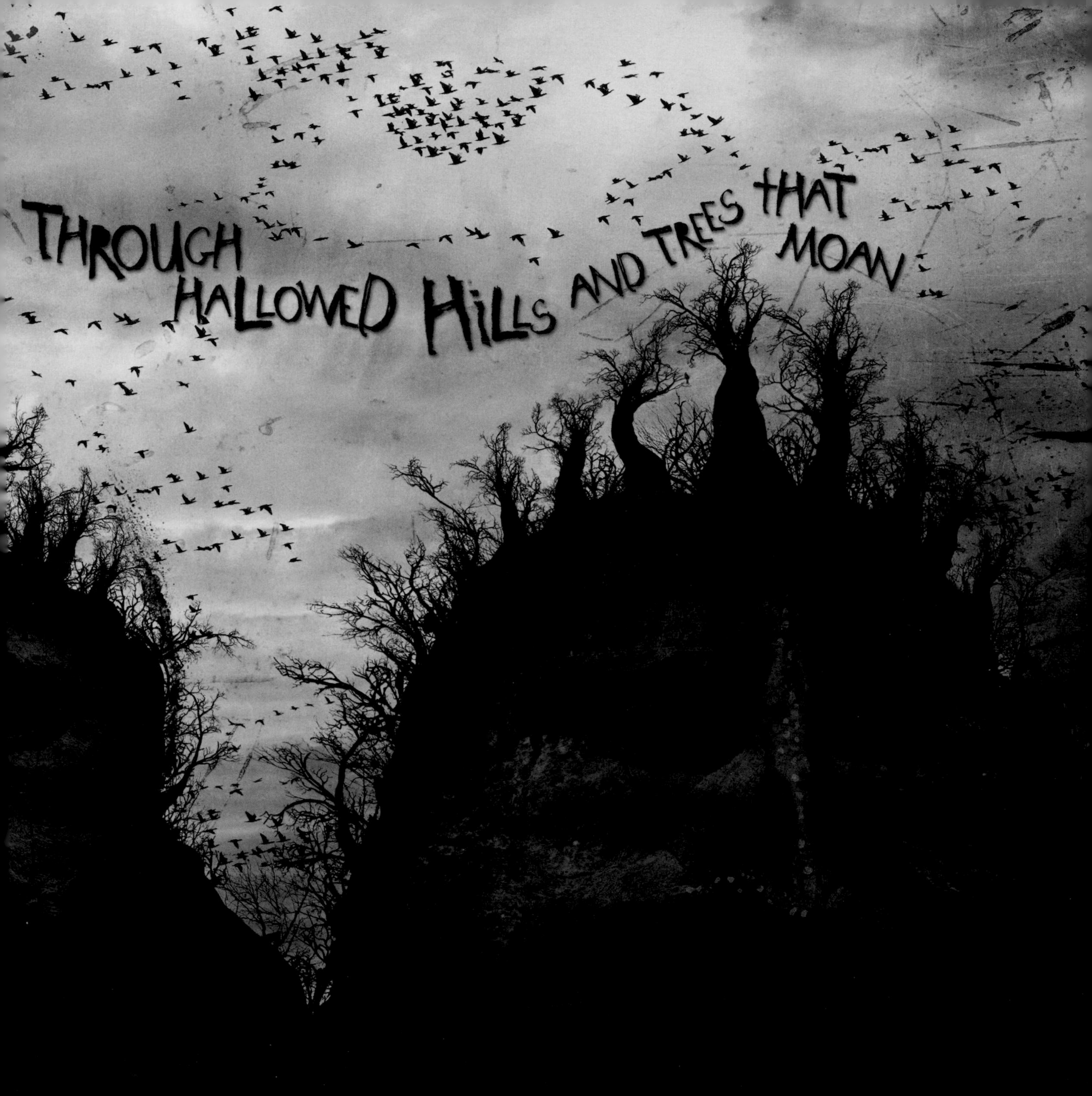
THROUGH HALLOWED HILLS AND TREES THAT MOAN

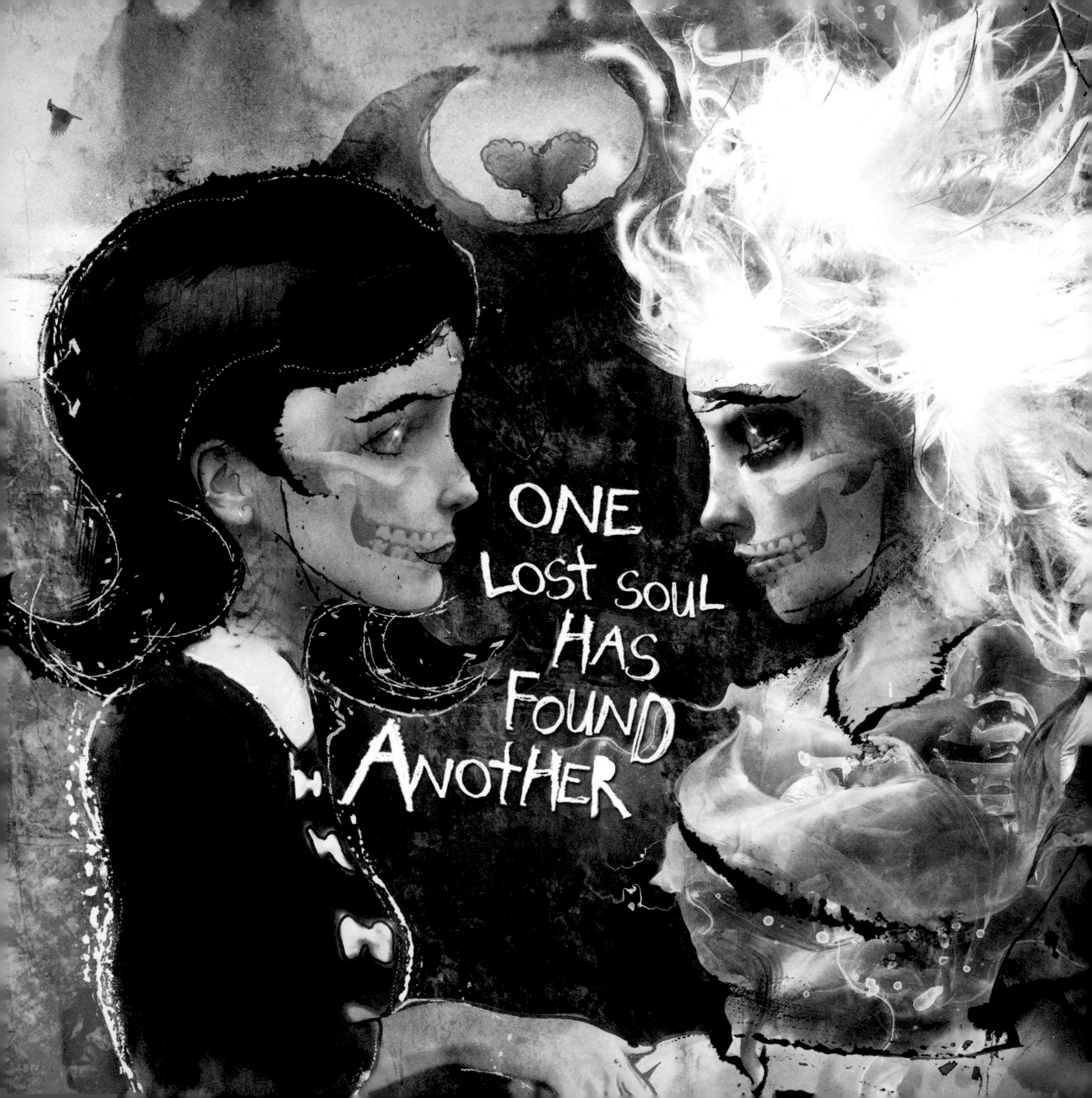
ONE
Lost soul
HAS
FOUND
ANOTHER

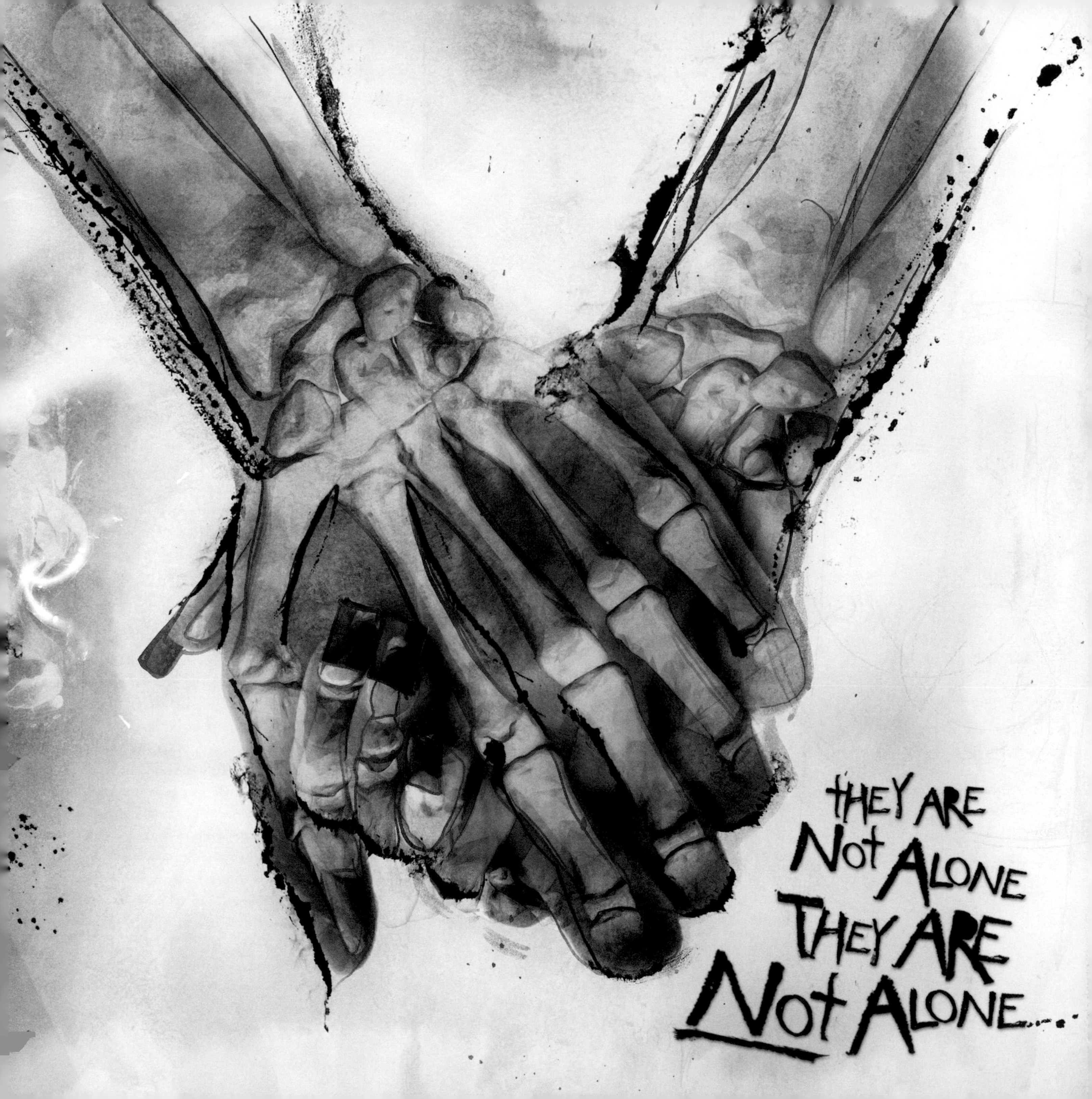
THEY ARE
NOT ALONE
THEY ARE
NOT ALONE...

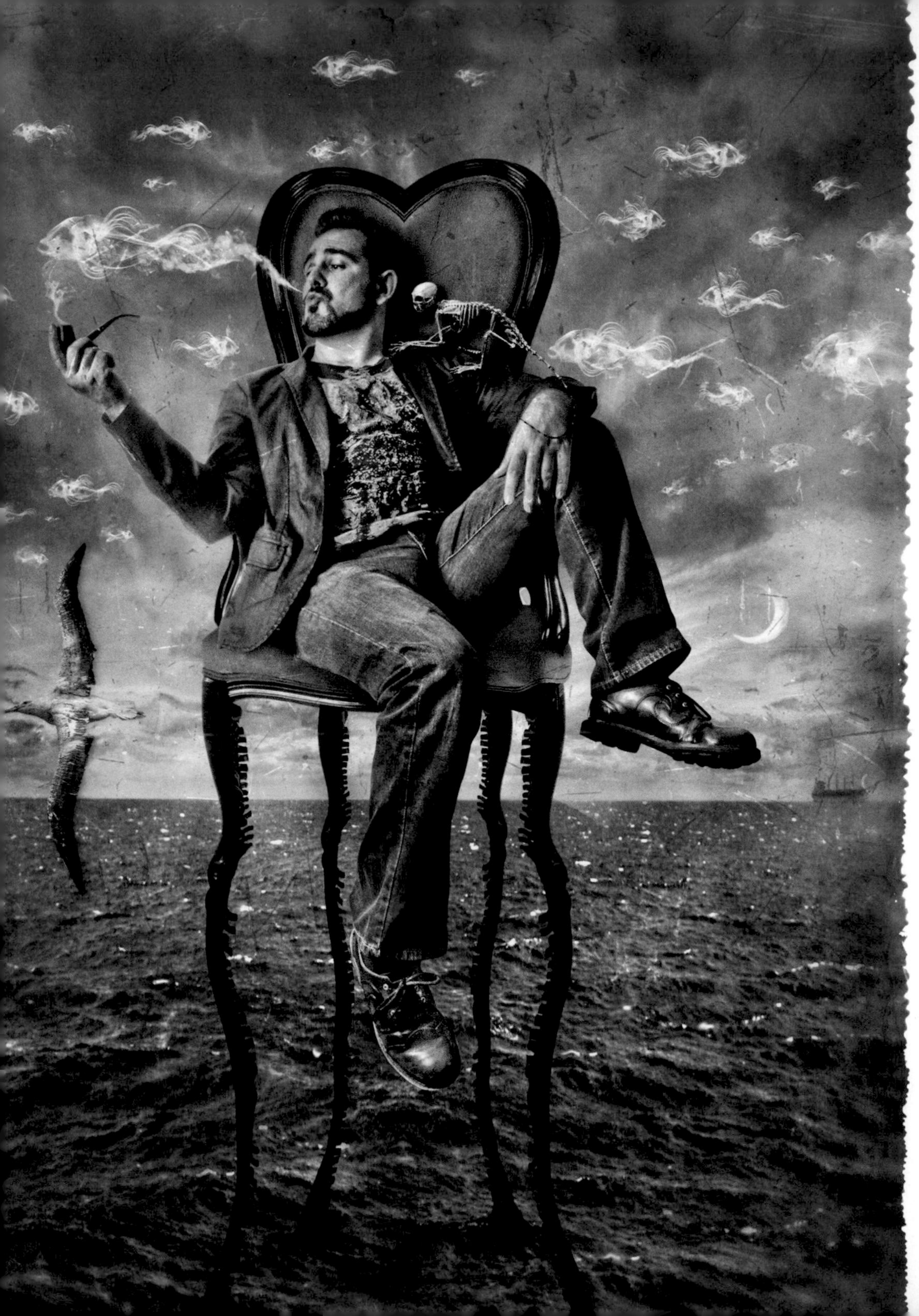

Vincent Marcone

"My Pet Skeleton" is the pseudonym for the award-winning graphic artist Vincent Marcone. This curious-sounding epithet caught on, crept in and slowly replaced his own name. As "My Pet Skeleton," Vincent catapulted to early success when his work and online worlds caught the attention of David Bowie, Guillermo Del Toro, Clive Barker, and the Godfather of Goth himself, Peter Murphy. His particular approach to painting album covers, and directing music videos has earned him awards from places as diverse as the Emmys, the Junos and even a Cannes Film Festival nomination for his short film "The Facts in the Case of Mister Hollow."

Vincent developed his unique style by combining his affection for the 600-year-old art of intaglio printmaking with his love of computer graphics. Early in his studies he would scrape and etch and carve his images onto zinc plates of all shapes and sizes, then send them hurtling through antiquated hand-turned presses. This experience and love of an old world aesthetic is what sets him apart from other digital artists. He handles his digital paintings as he handled his etchings, focusing in on the line work and meticulously placing each pixel to convey a sense of mood and ambiance. Drawing from a personal library of over 500 original textures (each created with metal plates and hand-wiped inks) Marcone uses his computer to fuse together media of all sorts to create imagery that is part of a larger story.

Vincent lives in Kitchener, Ontario where he is currently painting new pictures and crafting new tales. This is his very first book.

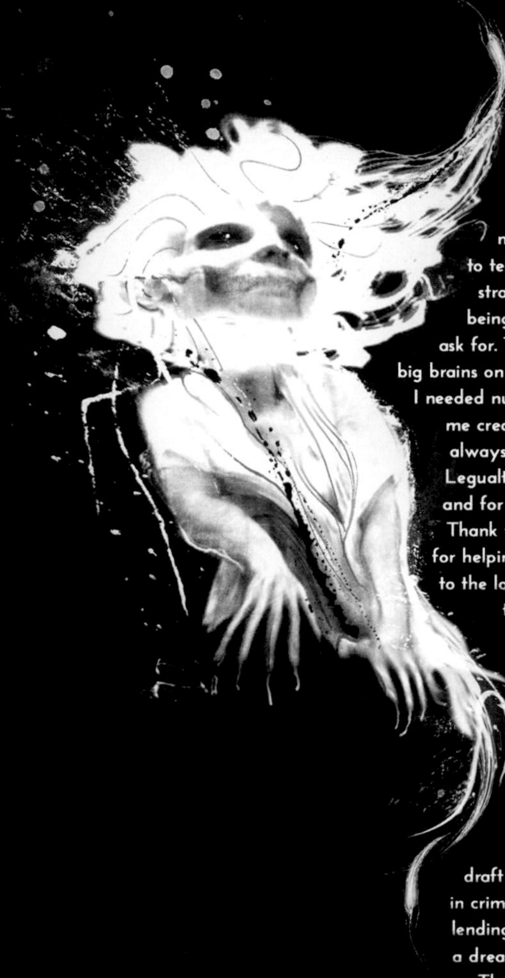

Thank You

Thank you to my Mother who shared countless magical tales with me as a child and sealed them with a goodnight kiss. Thank you to my Father who gave me the confidence to tell my own strange tales and share my own strange art. Thank you to Carolyn Forde, for being the most supportive agent an artist could ask for. Thank you to Natalie MacNeil for lending her big brains on marketing and strategy and for nudging me when I needed nudging. Thank you to Rodrigo Gudino for offering me creative advice and insightful critiques, you were always just a phone call away. Thank you to Sarah Legualt, for being an encouraging friend throughout and for inspiring the face of Miss ParaNorma herself. Thank you to Zak Hannah and Matthew Piotrowski for helping me process the storyboards and contributing to the layout and typography of this book. Thank you to Sandra Kasturi and Brett Savory for providing a wondrous creepy home for spooky stories like my own to take residence. Thank you to Samantha Beiko, editor extraordinaire, and also to Kelsi Morris, for helping shepherd the project forward. Thank you to Janine White who read the very first draft years ago and has been a creative partner in crime ever since. Thank you to Peter Murphy for lending your magical voice to the short film, it was a dream come true to work with you in the studio. Thank you to all my friends and family who offered encouraging smiles and enthusiastic words along the way. And certainly not least, thank you to Eric Martin for your patience, your calm and your loving heart. Each red cardinal is dedicated to you.

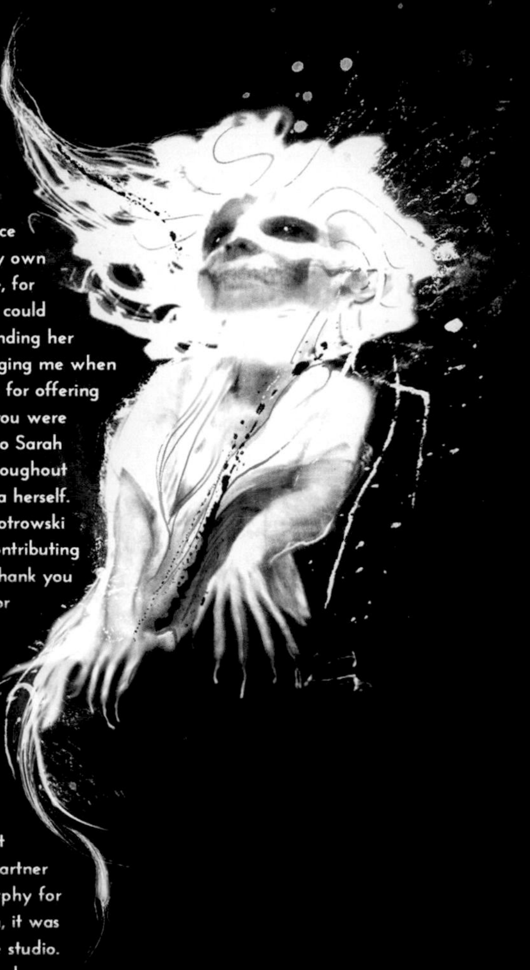

FIRST EDITION

The Lady ParaNorma © 2015 Vincent Marcone

Distributed in Canada by
PGC Raincoast Books
300-76 Stafford Street
Toronto, ON M6J 2S1
Phone: (416) 934-9900
e-mail: info@pgcbooks.ca

Distributed in the U.S. by
Diamond Comic Distributors, Inc.
10150 York Road, Suite 300
Hunt Valley, MD 21030
Phone (443) 318-8500
e-mail: books@diamondbookdistributors.com

Library and Archives Canada Cataloguing in Publication

Marcone, Vincent, author, illustrator
The Lady ParaNorma / Vincent Marcone.

Issued in print and electronic formats.
ISBN 978-1-77148-195-3 (pbk.)   ISBN 978-1-77148-196-0 (pdf)

        1. Graphic novels. I. Title.

PN6733.M363L34 2015   741.5'971   C2015-903044-7
                                            C2015-903045-5

CHIZINE PUBLICATIONS

Toronto, Canada

www.chizinepub.com

info@chizinepub.com

Proofread by Sandra Kasturi and Brett Savory

Layout by Samantha Beiko
Graphic Design by Vincent Marcone, Zak Hannah, Matthew Piotrowski

Canada Council   Conseil des arts
for the Arts   du Canada

We acknowledge the support of the Canada Council for the
Arts which last year invested $20.1 million in writing and
publishing throughout Canada.

ONTARIO ARTS COUNCIL
CONSEIL DES ARTS DE L'ONTARIO

an Ontario government agency
un organisme du gouvernement de l'Ontario

Published with the generous assistance of the Ontario Arts
Council

Printed in Canada

Watch the short film narrated by Peter Murphy here:
MYPETSKELETON.COM/FILMS

Download your FREE "Lady ParaNorma" digital gifts here:
MYPETSKELETON.COM/TREATS

DID YOU FIND ALL THE CARDINALS?

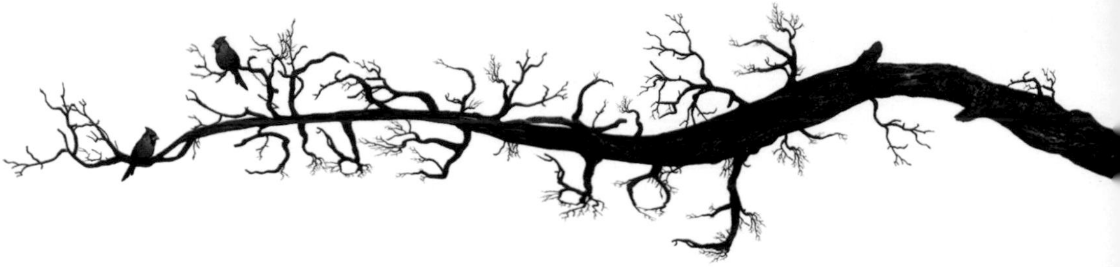

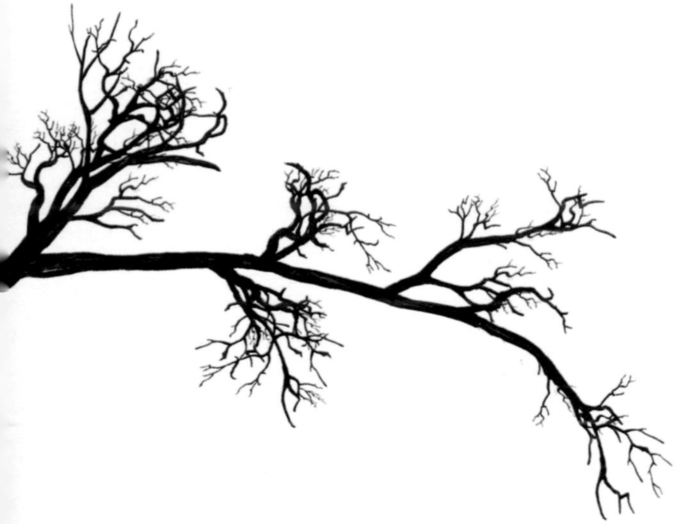

Sometimes together
Sometimes apart
Two birds of a feather
Share the same heart

On every page
Inside of this book
A cardinal hides
You just have to look...

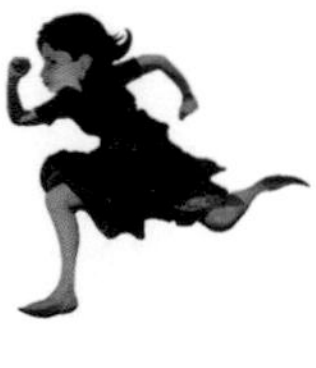